180°_{to}
Freedom

Break Free – and Change the Direction of Your Life

180°
to
Freedom

Break Free – and Change the Direction of Your Life

Renay West

Aljaba Producciones
Año 2012
Buenos Aires, Argentina

aljabaproducciones

180º to Freedom. Break Free – and Change the Direction of Your Life
Renay West

First Edition, August 2012
Aljaba Producciones
www.aljabaproducciones.com

Design: deselgraf@yahoo.com.ar

ISBN 978-987-28160-4-9

Dedication

To my Lord and Savior, Jesus Christ, who pulled me up out of a pit of hopelessness and despair and has filled my life with good things. He's been a Father and a friend to me. I could not imagine my life without Him.

> I waited patiently for the Lord; he turned to me and heard my cry.
> He lifted me out of the slimy pit, out of the mud and mire; he set my feet on a rock and gave me a firm place to stand.
> He put a new song in my mouth, a hymn of praise to our God.
> —Psalm 40:1-3

> Lord, you have assigned me my portion and my cup; you have made my lot secure.
> The boundary lines have fallen for me in pleasant places; surely I have a delightful inheritance.
> You have made known to me the path of life; you will fill me with joy in your presence, with eternal pleasures at your right hand.
> —Psalm 16:5, 6, 11

Acknowledgements

Thank you, Mom, for demonstrating unwavering love for the Lord. Your faithfulness, prayer life and consistent words of encouragement have forever marked my life.

Thank you, Graciela Gimenez, for your friendship. You are the sister I never had. Thank you for walking, working and dreaming with me in the ministry of Aguas de Sanidad. It would not have been the same without you, friend. Thank you, as well, for encouraging me to write this book!

Thank you, Darla Caldwell, for being such a true friend and for cheering me on in all of my dreams. Your friendship has been a hug from God.

I owe a debt of gratitude to the following people whose commitment and labor of love made this book a reality: Laura Bermudez (editor, Argentina), Larisa Grams (translator, Spanish version), Ilona Hadinger (editing, English version) and Beverly Shay (editing, English version). From my heart—thank you!

To all of my Argentine friends, who, truthfully, have become like family to me—thank you for letting me walk alongside you, and for walking with me. Go Boca!

About The Author

Renay West was born in Houston, Texas. She is an ordained minister and a graduate of Southwestern Assemblies of God University. She has served in various pastoral and pioneering ministry roles for the past 20 years.

She worked for several years in major-market Christian radio as an air personality. She last worked as Assistant Promotions/Public Relations Director and on-air personality at Houston's KSBJ Radio.

Renay speaks both Thai and Spanish, having graduated from linguistic institutes in Bangkok, Thailand, and Costa Rica, Central America.

From 1997 – 2005, she served as Area Media Ministries Director for Peninsular Asia (Thailand, Cambodia, and Myanmar), as well as compassion ministries coordinator. Her duties included the planning and construction of media studios, training of personnel, and creative director of media ministries projects geared towards reaching Buddhists and Muslims in the region. As Compassion Ministries Coordinator, Renay worked closely with Thai project leaders serving as liaison connecting the projects and their needs to foreign sponsors. She served with two children's home projects—one a home for children orphaned by AIDS, and the other a home in northern Thailand for rescued or at-risk child sex trade victims.

In 2006, Renay made the move to Buenos Aires, Argentina,

where she founded Aguas de Sanidad (Healing Waters) ministry in early 2007. Aguas de Sanidad (ADS) ministry not only functions as a freedom and healing ministry, but also works alongside other social foundations whose focus is family violence, child sexual abuse and exploitation. She and her team opened the Aguas de Sanidad Ministry Center in downtown Buenos Aires, where, alongside the Pablo Besson Foundation, they work extensively with victims and victimizers in small group settings, classes and one-on-one counseling. Renay and the ADS team have taken their conferences throughout Argentina, Latin America and Europe, ministering deliverance and healing to thousands.

Renay is a gifted communicator and travels extensively bringing a prophetic message of hope, freedom and transformation. She currently resides in Buenos Aires, Argentina with her amazing miniature schnauzer, Oliver.

Table of Contents

PROLOGUE

It is with immense joy that I write these lines, knowing that soon many will be able to enjoy the material in this book.

Over the past years, I've had the opportunity of getting to know Renay, of observing her love for the countries of southeast Asia and listening to her stories and anecdotes from the years in which she was a missionary to Thailand. I've also been able to see first-hand what God is doing through her in Argentina and other parts of the world where we've preached and taken the message of *Aguas de Sanidad* (Healing Waters) ministry. I never get tired of listening to the message God has placed on her heart for this generation.

This is not just another book. Among these words, you will find someone's life—their story, their road map. Above all, you'll be able to observe God's power transforming the most adverse realities. In the natural, given all of the circumstances involved, it would have been impossible to make any progress or to find a way out.

This book presents a message that will transform the way you see God. Nothing can prevent what He has prepared. As the Word says, nor height, nor depth, nor any other created thing, will be able to separate us from the love of God, which is in Christ Jesus our Lord. Only ignorance of what He has given you and of the potential He has placed in your life will separate you from all of the good things that are at your disposal to be experienced. Within these pages, one can begin to understand God's divine purposes for His children; in this case, for Renay's life. When a seed falls on good soil, even if it's in the midst of difficult times or circumstances that are not ideal, it will still produce something great. It causes what was hidden to emerge, to grow, and ultimately to bear fruit that stands the test of time.

The material in this book is a treasure God has given for this moment. I am confident that it's a prophetic word for our time that sheds light on different spiritual truths, exposing strongholds. I enjoyed reading the chapters while they were being written and I can't wait to see this book in peoples' hands. I know it will bring revelation and light to many areas of your life.

Topics such as spiritual inheritance, generational curses, healing, freedom, deliverance, transformation and recovery from wounds caused by childhood sexual abuse or domestic violence are not very popular. These are areas in which many people find themselves at an impasse. They have no idea how to resolve these issues, and feel hopeless in their plight to move forward with their lives. Not everyone is prepared to address these issues from a spiritual perspective, and lack the understanding necessary to bring freedom.

My desire is that the power of God will surprise you by giving you the answers you have been waiting for as you read this book. My prayer is that this will affect your entire life—that your spirit, soul and body may be transformed. That it won't just affect you but that others may also be healed, liberated and transformed through you.

Transformed persons are the ones who can affect change

in others. These changes will encompass their family, community, church, city and nation.

Enjoy this time of reading and ministry, and allow God to do a deep work in your life.

Graciela Giménez
PASTORAL COUNSELOR, SPEAKER AND WRITER

Introduction

So, when I thought about writing a book, I thought of a thousand reasons why I should not do it. It was fear, and insecurity. Definitely insecurity! I wondered if you, the reader, would be bored. I wondered if I really had something worthy of putting into print. I wondered if I could really give adequate expression to the deep workings of the Holy Spirit in my inner life: This excruciating, exhilarating journey from absolute devastation and emotional ruin to standing and executing life with authority and confidence that God truly, without hesitation or reserve, loves me completely.

I don't think I can convey all of the reasons why I felt compelled to write this book. But if I had to pin it down to one major reason it would be the deep conviction that we can make a difference in our generation and in the ones to come. But only if we share; only if we speak instead of remaining silent; only if we will be transparent about our own struggles so that the next generation can be aware of the pitfalls.

Change: That's what this book is about—more than anything else! It's about a generation inheriting the strongholds of their father's generation (or culture, environment). It's about that same generation being willing to search for answers and finding keys to break from inherited limits in order to, in turn, leave a legacy for the coming generation, rather than the disaster they inherited or fell into.

Can we change our history? No, we cannot. But in a *spiritual* sense—we can absolutely change the aftermath! In other words, our background *is* what it *is*. But, the Spirit of the Lord *in us* gives us the authority and the right to cause unsubmitted areas to submit and be transformed.

My Story

Throughout my growing up years, I always felt like there was something wrong with me. I felt ugly. I felt unlovable. I felt like a failure as a daughter, and as a young woman. I had this nagging feeling of guilt almost constantly. I would later suffer from horrific panic attacks in my adult years. There were many reasons for those things. Not the least of which were the conflicts that existed between my family's public and private life in my growing up years.

I was raised in a minister's home. Many may have thought we were an incredibly happy family. And, there were happy moments. But the reality was that we lived with a well-kept secret in our private life: family violence. Were there beatings? Yes. There were times when I could not dress out for physical education or sports because my legs and body were covered with welts (sometimes bloody ones) and bruises. I remember a beating that I got when I was two years old because I couldn't swallow a vitamin. I was yanked out of my baby chair and taken to my room. I was told I would be spanked until I took the vitamin. I couldn't breathe. I was face down on my bed with my bare bottom and legs exposed to a leather belt. During the beating, I would occasionally be yanked up and asked if I had taken the vitamin yet. It was always lying there on the bed, having fallen out of my mouth while I was struggling to escape the lashings of the belt. Finally, the vitamin fell out of my mouth and rolled, unnoticed, under the bed. That saved me from further beating that day as I lied and said I had swallowed it.

There were other incidents that would leave their marks on me, as well. When I was four years old, and we were crossing a suspension bridge at the Royal Gorge Canyon Park in Colorado, I sat down on the bridge because I was afraid of falling. The bridge was creaking in the wind. The river in the canyon below looked like a small squiggly line because we were so high up. When it was noticed that I was afraid and had sat down, I felt reassuring arms pick me up. The security only lasted a few seconds. I screamed and flailed around hysterically, as my arms were pried away, and I was lifted up over the edge of the bridge and held out over the open air. The person laughed, while my mom screamed hysterically and I cried uncontrollably. This was an incident that would repeat itself every time we visited the canyon. Fear of sudden trauma was something that I would deal with well into my adult years.

The atmosphere always vacillated between yelling and screaming and so thick you could slice-it-with-a-knife silent tension, which often drove me to my bed where I remember many times trembling uncontrollably. By the time I was 14 years old, I was being treated for stomach ulcers.

Living with a violent person in the home is like living with a ticking time bomb. You never know when or why the bomb explodes. And, if you are thinking, *Why don't you just disarm it?* Forget about it. You can't disarm it. Remember how in the movies the bombs always have a red and a blue wire? The person at least has a 50/50 shot at disarming it and saving his own life. But with a violent person, there are no wires!

No red wire. No blue wire. You can hear the ticking through the tension-building silence that always precludes an explosion. You learn to live very vigilantly to avoid any thing that could unintentionally set off the bomb. You are careful about how you speak and how you answer, and even how you walk through the room.

I had another secret. I lived with it for years. It was the secret of childhood sexual abuse. A man violated me at 10 years of age. The devastation took place in my own bedroom — in my own bed. I had to go back to that bed that very night. This man was a part of a family evangelistic team. So, after being sexually violated by him, I had to see him on the platform. This group was at our church for several weeks holding nightly services. After the initial abuse at my house, where I was home alone at the time, he even forced me inside some of the Sunday school classrooms in the church, repeatedly abusing me during the duration of their time there. I remember my personality changing almost overnight. I remember a dark cloud coming over my emotions. I remember believing the words of the pedophile when he told me, "You did something very bad today." He threatened me into silence. I felt filthy. I felt so ugly. I believed I had been born broken, and that there was no fix. My self-blame ended in self-hatred. My definition of self was formed through incidents outside of my control. I did not understand that I did not have to let those things define me and set the boundaries for the way I would live life.

These are just some of the things that shaped my life from the time I was a child. I believed the lies abuse, rejection and violence spoke to me. They were lies of the enemy. But when we believe a lie, it becomes just as powerful as truth. We buy into it, and it holds us captive to its limits and control.

At twenty years of age, God intervened in my life in a powerful way. I had an experience with Him like I had never had before. I had planned on taking my own life that night. But instead, I started a new one! There was an immediate transformation inside of me. No outside circumstance had changed, but the lies of the enemy were broken off of me and exposed so that I could begin pursuit of total healing and restoration. The term 'born-again' really describes what that night was like for me. I felt like I finally had the opportunity to become the person I was born to be.

So now maybe you understand a little bit more why I wrote this book. It's a guidebook—to fighting. It's a guidebook on overcoming. It's a guidebook on recognizing the spiritual strongholds behind our behavior. It's a guidebook on how to pull those strongholds down. I will not let strongholds of my lineage, nor of my own past, determine who I am or the future I will or will not have.

Purifying The Mantle

Jeremiah 2 is the account of the prophet's first assignment—the first message he was to deliver from the Lord to His people. God was laying this charge to the next generation:

> *What fault did your fathers find in me, that they strayed so far from me?* They did not ask, 'Where is the LORD, who brought us up out of Egypt and led us through the barren wilderness, through a land of deserts and rifts, a land of drought and darkness, a land where no one travels and no one lives?' I brought you into a fertile land to eat its fruit and rich produce. But you came and defiled my land and made my inheritance detestable. The

priests did not ask, 'Where is the Lord?'...(vs. 8) Therefore I bring charges against you again, declares the LORD. And I will bring charges against your children's children"

—JEREMIAH 2:5-8A, 9

"But you came and *defiled My land* and *made My inheritance destestable."* What a statement! *The defiling of a spiritual inheritance!* In verse 31, He continues to call out to this generation of sons and daughters—saying, "You of *this generation, consider the Word of the LORD...*"

As I read these passages, I felt so stirred in my spirit! I see within those lines the silhouette of my own history—and the history of thousands of others who have attended our ministry conferences and events—who have related their stories to my team and me.

Many of us feel that we inherited a defiled mantle—a spiritual inheritance that was stained or marred by failure or generational curses and sin. You may feel that, even from the time you were a child, you were set up for failure and not success. But even if that is the case, just as the Lord spoke to 'this generation' in Jeremiah, I believe He is speaking to *our* generation today, showing us that things defiled by one generation, can be restored by another.

History is full of both tragic and heroic stories demonstrating the influence of one generation over another. Generational influence is illustrated best in the biblical custom of the passing of one's mantle (cloak) to another, like Elijah did with Elisha. But, I wonder what would have happened had Elisha never picked up the mantle of Elijah? There would have been something that remained in the waiting: A spiritual inheritance, an increase, and the gift of living life at a whole new level.

Elisha was a person determined to break out of the limits of his own lineage. Elisha was proactive with regard to his future. In reality, he was nothing more than the servant of a prophet. He was a student of the Spirit only by virtue of having watched someone else live it—but *watching* had given him a deep craving for something more. By his natural inheritance, or, circumstances, he should have been plowing away in his family field. But he chose to pursue something greater. He *chose* to pick up that mantle. He chose to believe for something bigger than his background. He chose to change the course of his lineage and life!

My mother always instilled in me a feeling of divine purpose —even through years when I did not want her to do so—all of those early morning sermons she would preach to me as I sat sleepy-eyed eating my Cheerios! So when I finally surrendered myself to the Lord, I knew that God had a mantle for my life — there was something greater that He had planned for me, including the gift of living life at another level.

But the deeper I went with the Lord, the more I began to recognize problem areas in my life. It was frustrating. In my journey with Him, repetitive issues began to surface. I longed to recover lost years and even the lost me that somehow got displaced through my years of creating an image that, I thought, would serve to protect me from being further hurt or abused. I had built my life and personality around a gaping wound, an unresolved inner life. So, although I was full of passion for the things of God, full of zeal to be used by God—full of hope that the mantle He had placed before me would actually fit, I also knew that I had many deep inner needs crying out for resolution.

I tried my best to pray against those areas of weakness. I used every prayer formula known to mankind! I shouted at those things—I declared, I rebuked, I renounced—I honestly hated those things that were keeping me from wholeness and total freedom. They were preventing me from becoming who I wanted to become, preventing me from feeling at peace with God, with myself and with others. I needed the Holy Spirit to reveal to me the roots of those issues.

It seemed that none of my rebuking and renouncing of those behaviors and attitudes was effective. At that time, in 1998, I determined to fast and pray and get before God *until*: Until breakthrough. Until I had answers. Until something changed. That decision would be another turning point in my life. The first Scripture the Lord showed me on the first day of my week-long fast was Jeremiah 33:3, "Call unto me and I will answer you and I will *show you* (reveal to you, make known to you) great and unsearchable (unknown, hidden) things which you know not."

In the New Living Translation, Jeremiah 33:3, 6-7, 10-11 says:

> Ask me and I will tell you some remarkable secrets about what is going to happen here... The time will come when I will heal Jerusalem's (your) wounds and give it (you) prosperity and peace. I will restore the (your) fortunes of Judah and Israel and rebuild their (your) cities (inner life). This is what the LORD says: You say, 'This land (my life) has been ravaged, and the people and animals have all disappeared.' Yet in the empty streets of Jerusalem (in your inner desolate places) and Judah's other towns,

there will be heard once more the sounds of joy and laughter. The joyful voices of bridegrooms and brides will be heard again, along with the joyous songs of people (you and others who witness what I'm about to do in you) bringing thanksgiving offerings to the LORD. They will sing, 'Give thanks to the LORD Almighty, for the LORD is good. His faithful love endures forever!' For *I will restore* the prosperity of this land (your life)… says the LORD.

If you have felt, like I did, that you have hit an impasse and cannot seem to advance in your spiritual walk with the Lord, or, in your character and other areas of your life, don't be discouraged. Allow God to use that frustration to motivate you to fight for change.

Each of us has a choice to make. We will choose to let injustice or the failures of self or others set the boundaries of our lives, or we can choose something greater than our background and our history. We can change the trajectory of our life. May we *choose* to take up the mantle as Elisha did with the mantle of Elijah. Let's pick up the mantle of something greater—let's draw back with all of our might and with it strike the waters that lie like an impossibility before our lives and cry out for the God of our fathers to make Himself known to *us*, to our generation and to the generation of our children! May He restore from brokenness and break the cycle of sin. May we pass on something *greater* than we received!

This book is a record of my journey to restoration from brokenness and despair. My deep desire is that the key elements and Scriptures the Holy Spirit worked and revealed to me in my journey will serve to help, encourage and carry you further along in yours. If you have longed for the *freedom* to heal, to change and to move forward to something greater, I believe the key principles you will find in this book will give you courage to act for change in your life. May the fear of remaining the same be greater than our fear of change!

CHAPTER 1

SPIRITUAL INHERITANCE

It amazes me when I hear someone who has no relationship with the Lord expressing spiritual principles without even realizing what they are saying or why they feel the way they do. It's kind of exciting to see spiritual laws at work to the point that even those who have no knowledge of the things of the Spirit recognize that something greater than what they see in the natural is at work.

How many times have you watched a talk show or heard individuals talking about their habits, addictions or behavior in light of the habits, addictions or behavior of their parents? Even those with no understanding of God's word understand that there is a link (behavioral sciences) between our mindset and the mindset of our fathers' generation, even traced back to multiple generations. Some say this behavior is 'learned'; some call it generational curses.

There are two major factors which have played into a certain resistance in the church regarding the subject of generational curses: One is extreme doctrine which has taken an element of truth and stretched it way beyond biblical bounds. The second major factor is secular psychology, which essentially blames the behavior of the child on influencing elements in childhood, specifically and most often, the parents.

There is an element of truth in each of these schools of thought. In fact, we can see threads of these ideas in Scripture—but with an incredible balance. I was raised hearing of the evils of psychology. I was also raised to believe the whole idea of generational curses was heresy. And, in my opinion, there are many whose doctrine regarding this subject is unscriptural. Having said that, I also believe there's a lot of wisdom in the old saying, "Don't throw the baby out with the bathwater." As I began to dig deeper and ask the Holy Spirit to give me insight into some of the strongholds in my own life, I was amazed at what I found.

Hosea 4:6 says, "My people are destroyed for lack of *knowledge*." Knowledge, in this Scripture, refers to understanding and discernment. It's not the big evils, which keep us from living totally free—sometimes it's simply the lack of knowledge, the lack of knowing our spiritual rights and position that keeps us under the enemy's thumb.

Earlier, I mentioned a fast that I went on in 1998. It was a turning point in my life. I knew I was dealing with a lot of symptoms of deep strongholds in my inner life, and I was sick of them. I had heard sermons, prayed through at the altar a billion times, applied every prayer formula known to mankind, but still knew the roots remained. Little did I know that when I closed the door to my house that day in 1998 to begin that fast, I was embarking on a journey through the Scriptures such as I had never known before. I was determined to get answers from the Lord. Fasting was key. (More on that in another chapter)

The Lord impressed upon me the Scripture in Jeremiah 33:3—Call unto me, and I will answer you, and I will show you great and mighty things, which you know not. In another version, it uses the words unsearchable, hidden things. God had my attention. The Holy Spirit took me on a journey in the Word—He revealed so many Scriptures to me and began to speak to me about the issues with which I was so preoccupied. I remember calling my mom several times, asking, "Mom—was this or that particular sin or stronghold an issue somewhere in our family tree—or is it currently an issue?" I remember her pausing and thinking about it and then saying something like, "As a matter of fact, yes. How did you know that?" The Lord was answering me, and showing me *great and hidden* things that I did not know! I was beginning to understand that there was a strongman who had been trying to destroy our family for generations.

We all know there is a strongman—we know his name is Satan. But we forget how crafty he is. It's easy to forget, in our modern reality, that there is a very real spiritual war raging all around us. The enemy has an entire spiritual hierarchy (principalities and powers) at his discretion. I often say we would be astounded and shocked if the curtain that divides the visible from the invisible realm were to be drawn back for a moment. I believe we'd live life differently—we would be vigilant spiritually!

So, as my weeklong fast came to an end, the Lord had armed me with *knowledge (understanding) and discernment.* I began to take a closer look at what the Bible has to say about generational issues.

The first Scripture that I studied was Exodus 20:5: "You shall not bow down to them nor serve them. For I, the LORD your God, am a jealous God, <u>visiting the iniquity of the fathers upon the children to the third and fourth generations</u> of those who hate Me."

This is the Scripture commonly referred to when people speak about "generational curses." They site the part that I've underlined. If God were to have left us to the discretion of this single Scripture, we would be in bad shape! But God has always provided something incredibly important in the plan of redemption since the beginning of creation: *free will.* He hasn't left us helpless beneath the curse of the sins of our fathers. *He has provided for us.* Even in Old Testament times, He provided a way *out* from under the curse.

Deuteronomy 30:15, 19 says:

See, I have set before thee this day life and good, and death and evil; I call heaven and earth to record this day against you, that I have set before you life and death, blessing and cursing: therefore choose life, that both thou and thy seed may live.

Choose! To make a wise choice, we have to be well informed. First of all, we have to understand what we are dealing with. And we have to understand the consequences and price required of our options. Every generation has a choice to make.

When we talk about generational curses, what are we really talking about? It sounds so mystical, powerful and bigger than us! The phrase *generational curse* conjures up a feeling of being powerless and helpless regarding some spiritual tsunami force that is out to get us—one that can leave us feeling as if we have no choice in the matter, as if it is destined to overtake them.

Nothing could be further from the truth.

If the enemy can intimidate you into believing a lie, you will live beneath its limits, giving it power to define your reality. That's why Hosea 4:6 is so important! "My people were destroyed from lack of *knowledge*! John 8:32 tells us how *critical* knowledge is! "You shall *know* the truth and the truth shall set you free!" You have to *know* before freedom can come.

Here's a great example of a diabolical lie: "This is just the why I am. I've always been this way. My dad was this way." Or, "My mom was this way. Our family is just this way." Yeah. That's a great example of someone buying into the intimidation and lie of the enemy over their life!

A generational curse is nothing more than a *sin* that was committed at some point in the family line. A sin is an act of disobedience or an act that is displeasing to the Lord. Sin is displeasing to God primarily because it robs *us* of enjoying an unhindered relationship with Him!

When we talk about sin, it's important to understand that sin is more than just an act committed by a person. There is a *motivator* behind sin — his name is Satan. He does tempt. He does try to set people up for failure and destruction, aiming to destroy the purposes of God in each generation. In fact, the enemy never ceases to look for an entrance into every generation. Maybe the person who fell into that certain sin and propagated it in their family has since passed on. But, don't think for a minute that the enemy has forgotten his right to rule in that bloodline. For that reason we see sins repeated for generations in a family line. And, when the enemy has had the freedom to move about for generations in a family, through the open door that sin has afforded him, he will not easily relent his territory! This is why there exists such a fierce spiritual battle to administrate freedom and establish godly dominion in places and families where oppression has long had such free reign.

With Aguas de Sanidad, we clearly encounter generational strongholds on a regular basis. They are easy to identify as we sit and listen to the stories of men and women, boys and girls, week in and week out. I doubt that I've ever heard even one story that didn't involve a domino effect in the family. The enemy loves to bully entire families! With the stories we hear, strongholds are easily identified — a violent spirit — a spirit of rage and murder; a perverse spirit — incest, struggles with sexual perversion or sexual identity issues, sexual abuse; addictions to drugs and alcohol; a suicidal spirit — self-destructive behavior; mental illness — generational issues with bipolar, schizophrenia, etc. Understand that not every physical or spiritual issue is a demon or a spirit, but often a spiritual root is evident. There may not be a curse involved, but there's most definitely a stronghold in play!

When a person begins a relationship with God, the blood of Jesus destroys the *authority* of sin in the person's life. Yet remember, sin was more than an act. The enemy had a plan to destroy the life of the person through that sin! In other words, the enemy had a long-term strategy to dominate that person's life. Even after the sin is forgiven, the enemy will continue pestering, threatening and attempting to claim that territory — after all, he *previously* had legal rights to dominate there! If the person doesn't understand (have *knowledge*) their *right* to come out from under the enemy's threat and intimidation in certain areas of their life or character, they will continue living as though they aren't *legally* free (spiritually speaking).

A great analogy of this can be seen in U.S. history. Abraham Lincoln was a man ahead of his times. (Thank God for that!) He understood the evil of slavery, identifying its horrific consequences. If not abolished, it would destroy the nation. So, he stood up and went against the grain. He penned the Emancipation Proclamation, the first step toward abolition of slavery. This document, unveiled on September 22, 1862, immediately freed thousands of slaves. But in the South, specifically in Texas, the southern government and slave owners refused to speak of or publicize the executive order. It wasn't made public knowledge in Texas until almost three years later when, on June 19, 1865, General Gordon Granger read General Order No. 3 in Galveston, Texas. It read: "The people of Texas are informed that, in accordance with a proclamation from the Executive of the United States, all slaves are free."

That means that there were thousands of legally *free people* living as slaves for *years* after they had been freed! Legally they were free — but because they lacked the *knowledge* of their *rights* — they continued living under the label, the limits and the domination of slavery.

How many of us have experienced the same thing? We love God, we believe that Jesus died on the cross for our sins, but somehow we have continued under the yoke of slavery in certain areas of our hearts and lives. The threat of the enemy through that stronghold or area of your soul has you convinced that you are *not* free — at least not *there*—that's *his* land!

You see, when spiritual strongholds are left *unconfronted* generation after generation, their strength and the gravity of their consequences increase generationally. Their threat grows. They are bullies. Even as believers, we can become overwhelmed at the giant looming in front of us — we make a commitment to the Lord, but then when we want to affect change in our family and turn things around and honor God, that strongman raises his ugly head and roars in our ear convincing us of his *dominion* and the impossibility of casting him out of his territory!

This is the point where many Christians simply back down, convinced by the roar. They believe that the displayed *strength* of the enemy is evidence of his authority or right to be there. But the Bible says that the enemy is a liar, and the truth is not in him! As a blood-bought believer, you have the *authority* to uproot the *power* of the enemy in your life and in the life of your family. Jesus gave us authority over all the power of the enemy. ***Authority trumps power!*** I'm going to talk more in depth about our spiritual authority and rights in a later chapter.

We must remind the enemy that we are not culpable for the sins of our fathers! God does not lay their sin to our charge. But, we *are* called upon to draw a line in the sand and declare, "Up to here, but no further!" Will you be the one to change the direction of your lineage spiritually?

Our hope is in the promises, or the spiritual laws, which God put into affect through Jesus' blood and His resurrection. Romans 5:20 says that where sin abounds, grace abounds all the more! Where sin's root is deep, the grace of God goes deeper still!

Deuteronomy 7:9 tells us, "Know therefore that the LORD

thy God, he is God, the faithful God, which keepeth *covenant and mercy* with them that love him and keep his command-ments *to a thousand generations.*"

So we see that not only are there generational curses, there are also *generational blessings!* We have the opportunity to take dominion over the strongholds that have dominated our fam-ilies for generations. We also have the opportunity to change the course of our lineage — in other words, purify and sanc-tify what we leave as an inheritance for the next generation. The added bonus is the influence on *this* generation as well.

One of the best illustrations ever of a generational turn-around is found in Joshua chapter 7. What we see in this chapter is a new generation of Israelites that have crossed over the Jordan River and entered into the Promised Land. In so doing, they went further than their fathers ever had. These were the children of the disobedient generation that never claimed their inheritance. Why? Because their fear of the gi-ants was greater than their desire for the milk and honey. This new generation had been raised in the desert. They had paid the consequence of their parents' failure. I'm sure they were incredibly anxious to have the chance to turn things around and get out of that desert.

They enter into Canaan under Joshua's leadership, who gave them the plan—exactly as he had received instruction from the Lord—for a successful campaign to take posses-sion of their Promised Land. God explained the strategy for Jericho—they were to circle the city once a day for six days and then seven times on the seventh day. Finally, they were to shout with all their might when Joshua commanded them, after the priests sounded their trumpets. You know the story: The walls fell down. This new generation of Israelites went into the city and, according to the command that the Lord gave to Joshua, they destroyed everything in it, except for Rahab and her family members that were in her house at the time the walls fell. God had also told Joshua that they were not to take any of the goods of Jericho for themselves. Everything was to be destroyed.

The only problem was that not everyone obeyed what the Lord had instructed. One man disobeyed. A man named Achan found some things in the city that he simply could not resist. He was incredibly attracted to a Babylonian mantle (or cloak) that he found in the city. He also came across some silver and gold. I can understand his temptation to take the silver and gold, but come on — a mantle? Really?

Yes, really. It is very interesting what you find when you study the significance of the mantle. In biblical times, when one person passed their mantle to another person, there was an impartation. There was a transaction that took place. It meant that there was unity between those two people. Some have even referred to it as a spirit of adoption between the two. I'm talking about a soul tie or a spiritual bond. Some theologians suggest the recipient even took on the spirit, or the characteristics and tendencies, of the other. We can see this in the life of Elisha when he took up the mantle of Elijah. The company of prophets who watched the scene play out from a distance suddenly exclaimed, "Look, the spirit of Elijah is now resting on Elisha!" (II Kings 2:15).

The Baylonians were gifted at using colored and golden thread in the weaving of their mantles. Without a doubt the mantle that Achan saw was eye-catching.

But there was something else very significant about this mantle's origin. It was from Babylon. Babylon was the place where humanity decided to raise itself up to a position equal to God. They felt invincible. They had become self-reliant, rather than looking to God for their dependency. Babylon was the birthplace of idolatry, and certainly the poster child for spiritual pride. The spirit behind those attitudes was none other than Satan himself. It was the same spirit that rose up in the hearts of the generation of Israelites who God had delivered out of Egypt. It influenced their hearts and minds. Its aim was to drive them away from God. It was the same spirit intent on keeping them from taking hold of what God had purposed for them.

So here's Achan, in a sense, toying with the same spirit that destroyed his father. He grabs the mantle and also takes the silver and gold, and then returns to camp with the rest of the people.

Everyone was celebrating! It was a good day! It was a historic day! God had given them a great victory over Jericho!

Little did they know that even though the walls crumbled before them, a door had been thrown wide open to the enemy. An entire generation was about to be brought to a complete standstill.

Soon after their Jericho victory party, Joshua sent spies up to the next little town called Ai. The town was so small that, when the spies saw it, they came back and told Joshua, "Don't even bother sending up the whole army — look what we did to Jericho, a huge metropolitan city! Ai is so small, just send a few of us up, and we'll have it taken care of easily!" Such confidence!

So, that's exactly what Joshua did. The men went up fearlessly, but came back melting with fear! They could not believe it! They had been defeated and publicly shamed by a small band of untrained men from a little place called Ai! Soon, the word spread through the camp. Everyone, including Joshua, began to tremble and question the validity of their call and God's favor. Defeat will do that to you. You fail, and your entire perspective changes. Suddenly, your confidence disappears and even your *thinking* changes! You question everything you were recently passionate and sure about!

Joshua tore his clothes and got before the Lord. He began to question God. He said, "God, why did you ever bring us across the Jordan? Was it just to deliver us into the hands of the giants of this land? Did I really hear from You? If only we had been content to stay back on the other side of the Jordan! You know what will happen now? All of the enemies of this land will hear about our embarrassing defeat and they will consider us beatable! They will come and surround us and wipe us out! God, are you listening? Are you here with us? What will you do, then, for Your great name?" Joshua was in essence saying, "We are marked by *Your* name! This is about *You*! It's about Your promises! Your Covenant! Your reputation!" He was throwing it all back on God's shoulders!

When I read that Scripture I can hear my own voice and the countless times I have gotten before the Lord like that! If I hadn't been so desperate at those times, it might even be funny to me right now! I truly *was* desperate! But, like Joshua, I was blind to the real problem! The issue was not that the Israelites were incapable. It wasn't that God's promises weren't authentic. Or that He dangled some kind of unattainable carrot before them to get them to take a leap of faith in order to position them for failure. Nor was this a case of the sins of the father being visited on the children as they might have assumed. No, that sin was covered by their leap of faith and obedience in crossing over the Jordan and following Joshua (who is a type of Christ).

This was about one thing and one thing only: Somebody opened a door for the enemy giving him legal rights to disturb the forward momentum of God's plan for their lives. They were at a generational crossroads: Would they repeat the sins of the father?

God responds to Joshua and says, "Stand up, Joshua! Why are you down on your face like that? This is not some strange or unwarranted thing! Israel has sinned. That's why this happened! There is a hidden thing in the camp. The enemy has a foothold here because someone sowed something of the enemy into the camp! Tell the Israelites they will not be able to stand against their enemies, nor be established in the sight of their enemies, until they uproot and destroy it!"

In some versions the Bible names those hidden things as things devoted to destruction. God's will is never to destroy the *person* who has fallen into the grip or snare of sin. No. He is adamant about sin because He knows that it brings destruction to His creation — to you and to me! He calls us to destroy those things completely, uprooting them so that we ourselves won't be uprooted and destroyed! They are *devoted to destruction* so that their chains will not bind us.

The phrase, "You cannot stand against your enemies until you remove it" is so powerful! It was the phrase that shook me to action when I was trying to understand why I couldn't seem to stand consistently in certain areas of my life. It resounded loudly in my spirit — it was like a wake-up call to look a little deeper and ask God to expose whatever the stronghold was that kept me from standing against the enemy.

God exposed the hidden things when His people consecrated

(devoted) themselves to Him. Joshua called the people together, told them to prepare themselves for what the Lord was going to do. Tribe by tribe, clan by clan and finally, family by family, God began to eliminate and then pinpoint where the problem was. He called out Achan's family — the last family standing. And finally, Achan confessed. He said, "It is true! I have sinned against the Lord, the God of Israel. This is what I have done: When I saw in the plunder a beautiful robe from Babylonia, two hundred shekels of silver and a wedge of gold weighing fifty shekels, I coveted them and took them. They are hidden in the ground inside my tent, with the silver underneath." (Joshua 7:20, 21)

He said he *coveted* them. That word, *coveted,* literally means that he took pleasure in them; he *lusted* after them. There was something powerful that attracted him to those things. I believe it was the same spirit that seduced his fathers! It was that same generational hound looking for a way into this new generation. And, it found a way in — through the door opened by Achan's disobedience.

There was nothing mystical about it. It was not the result of a curse. He simply opened the door without considering the devastating consequence! Achan took hold of the same spirit that had defeated his fathers and introduced it into his generation. He sowed the seed of his enemy into his inheritance! He buried something toxic contaminating the land that God was trying to purify as an inheritance to him and his children and his children's children, even to a thousand generations! He opened up the ground beneath his dwelling and sowed a seed of destruction—and the seed quickly bore fruit.

Achan's sin didn't affect him alone. Sin does not honor boundaries. It's like a bomb. You may bury it in one tiny spot, but when it explodes, it wreaks havoc at a 360-degree radius. Many are affected.

Achan's entire family, his animals, and everything that belonged to him were brought before the Lord and all of the people and were destroyed that day. It was a day of spiritual abortion. Generations were aborted because of his actions. Listen — the devil *never* has our best interest at heart. Sin is pleasurable for a season — but how awful when that season ends. It leads to complete destruction.

The inspiring part of this story is found in the response of the rest of the people. After Achan was exposed, Joshua sent messengers to Achan's tent to remove the things Achan had buried. The Bible doesn't say that he told them to *run* to Achan's tent, but that's what they did. There was a *run* in their spirit! They had lived the consequences of disobedience once, and they were not willing to let it happen again. The entire generation came to a dead standstill until the hidden thing was removed. When, as a generation, they recognized the risk of repeating the sins of their fathers, they had an urgency in their spirit to confront that stronghold and uproot it completely. They ran!

So, where does one start in confronting a generational stronghold? The most important element is the atoning blood of the Lord Jesus. Exodus 12 says,

> Tell the whole community of Israel that on the tenth day of this month each man is to take a lamb for his family, one for each household. Then they are to take some of the blood and put it on the sides and tops of the doorframes of the houses where they eat the lambs. "On that same night I will pass through Egypt and strike down every firstborn of both people and animals, and

I will bring judgment on all the gods of Egypt. I am the LORD. The blood will be a sign for you on the houses where you are, and when I see the blood, I will pass over you. No destructive plague will touch you when I strike Egypt.

–EXODUS 12:3, 7, 12-13

The key to breaking strongholds that have been passed generationally is a spiritual transaction: Applying the blood of the Lamb to your house —your life! The blood breaks the curse (takes away a guilty 'verdict')—but there's still a strongman to deal with!

Matthew 12:29 talks about the strongman. *Or again, how can anyone enter a strong man's house and carry off his possessions unless he first ties up the strong man? Then he can plunder his house.*

In her book, *Break the Generation Curse,* Marilyn Hickey brings an insight I love. She says, "In this scripture *house* can mean *generation* (see Matt. 10:6). In order to break the curse of the generations behind us — their habits, their sins, their physical weaknesses—you have to go in and bind the strong man who has brought that curse from generation to generation.

So, who is this strong man? Satan, of course. The devil is the strong man. What do we have to do to him? We must bind him. And then what? We take the house—*or that generation*—away from him!"

We can apply the blood to our house, our generation! *The obedience of one has the power to bless even a thousand generations!* The turning point begins with applying the blood of Jesus to our lives — simply asking the Lord Jesus to cover our lives — all of it — past, present, and future, with His saving blood. *That simple transaction activates the blessing, favor and authority of God over your life.* This translates into the *authority* to confront the strongman and plunder his house, having what was stolen from you restored. Joel 2 tells us God even restores lost time: "I will restore the years…"

Too often, the enemy uses fear, terror and intimidation to keep us from even considering looking for the roots of strongholds, be it in our families or in our own life. When I went before God during my fast in 1998, I was, quite honestly, scared. What would I find by giving the Lord a chance to speak to me about…me. I thought maybe I'd have to endure years of counseling (and, by the way, I have greatly benefitted from godly counselors), or maybe I'd have to leave full-time ministry in order to deal with some of the big, bad wolves of my inner life. But as the Holy Spirit began to gently speak to my heart, I found that the biggest step was confronting the fear.

The devil is like the proverbial school ground bully — his biggest strength is his *bluff.* If you'll be brave enough to call him on it, you will have won half the battle simply by your willingness to let God look inside and guide you into truth — truth that will set you free from the chains (the bluff) of the enemy. The Holy Spirit is a gentleman. He will gently guide you and reveal to you "great and unsearchable things" which you know not. If there are things that need to be uprooted or things that need to be confronted spiritually, He will reveal those things to you when you seek Him.

In the next few chapters, I am going to give you several key principles for effective spiritual warfare. The most important element is what you will find in the next chapter — knowing *who* you are, and knowing your spiritual rights. Keep reading!

CHAPTER 2

THE BLESSING OF THE FATHER

Blessing means to *favor*, to prosper, or to identify—literally to *give* identity.

"God bless you!" How many times have we said that to someone? It's become a common greeting between believers and in church circles. We even sign our e-mails "Blessings!"

There is an entire historical background that we see in Scripture regarding the blessing. The blessing of the father was considered part of the firstborn son's inheritance, and was of equal or more importance than the monetary inheritance. The blessing, biblically, in the Old Testament, was the declaration of the favor and grace of God over the firstborn son.

Biblically and historically, the blessing was based on *who* the person was rather than in their works or accomplishments. In other words, the blessing was not a reward for works—you had to be *born* into it! In form, it was a prophetic declaration spoken over the life of the person and was given by the father to his firstborn. It was a prophetic utterance driven by the will of God and given under the direction of the Spirit of the Lord. It was given to the firstborn regardless of their failures or successes. It was not just words of encouragement or well-wishing, but was comprised of divine words which were backed by supernatural power for fulfillment. When the blessing was spoken, something was activated in the Spirit realm.

In the life of Isaac and his sons Jacob and Esau, the Bible gives us a clear example of just what import the spoken blessing carried. God Himself honored the words of the earthly father. Even when spoken in error — the act, the words, the declaration could not be reversed. When Isaac realized he had been deceived into blessing Jacob instead of his firstborn Esau, he said, "Who was it, then, that hunted game and brought it to me? I ate it just before you came, and I blessed *him—and indeed, he will be blessed!*" (Gen. 27:33).

The blessing of the father, as seen in the story of Isaac and his sons, is an Old Testament model of a New Testament truth, as seen in Romans 8:15-17:

> For you did not receive a spirit that makes you a slave again to fear, but you *received the Spirit of sonship* (adoption). And by him we cry, "Abba, Father." The Spirit himself testifies with our spirit that *we are God's children. Now if we are children, then we are heirs—heirs of God and co-heirs with Christ,* if indeed we share in his sufferings in order that we may also share in his glory.

When we come into relationship with our heavenly Father,

through His Son, that *spirit of adoption* makes us heirs—we become joint-heirs with Christ, having all the benefits, security, divine help, favor and grace, as a blood-born child would have. God wants us to enjoy the freedom and the benefits, both emotionally and spiritually, of sons and daughters.

We live in a lost generation— one in which the influence and role of the father is missing. Scores of this generation resent their history or the position into which they were born. A feeling of abandonment pervades. There's the feeling of not having a chance to be greater because of being born into something lesser. It's the feeling that says we don't stand a chance to go any farther than our fathers went. Many feel that they are destined to repeat the lack and the inabilities of their fathers. By using the term *fathers*, I'm referring to our fathers *and* our mothers, or whoever or whatever held the greatest influence over our lives, shaping our outlook and way of thinking. We are all products of our society, of our early childhood and its influencers. This is all true. But! There is a *spiritual law* that *frees us* from the natural law. There is a *blessing* that breaks the cycle and power of sin, limits and failures and sets forth and activates something divine and supernatural in our lives.

So, how did the blessing of the firstborn work? What areas did it touch in the recipient's life? Let's look at the blessing Isaac spoke over Jacob's life, keeping in mind that he was picturing Esau as he blessed Jacob.

Here's the scenario as Jacob entered his father's tent, deceiving him in order to gain the blessing:

> He went to his father and said, "My father." "Yes, my son," he answered. "Who is it?"
> Jacob said to his father, "I am Esau your firstborn. I have done

as you told me. Please sit up and eat some of my game so that you may give me your blessing."

Isaac asked his son, "How did you find it so quickly, my son?" "The LORD your God gave me success," he replied.

Then Isaac said to Jacob, "Come near so I can touch you, my son, to know whether you really are my son Esau or not."

Jacob went close to his father Isaac, who touched him and said, "The voice is the voice of Jacob, but the hands are the hands of Esau." He did not recognize him, for his hands were hairy like those of his brother Esau; so he blessed him. "Are you really my son Esau?" he asked. "I am," he replied.

Then he said, "*My son*, bring me some of your game to eat, so that I may give you my blessing." Jacob brought it to him and he ate; and he brought some wine and he drank. Then his father Isaac said to him, "Come here, *my son*, and kiss me."

So he went to him and kissed him. *When Isaac caught the smell of his clothes*, he blessed him and said, "Ah, the smell of *my son* is like the smell of a field that the LORD has blessed. May God give you of heaven's dew and of earth's richness— an abundance of grain and new wine. May nations serve you and peoples bow down to you. Be lord over your brothers, and may the sons of your mother bow down to you. May those who curse you be cursed and those who bless you be blessed."

After Isaac finished blessing him and Jacob had scarcely left his father's presence, his brother Esau came in from hunting.

–GEN. 27:18-30

There are three main areas that Isaac's blessing emphasized to his son: Identity, image, and the capacity for increase.

Identity

From the beginning, we see Isaac establishing *identity* through his words to his son. If you'll notice in verses 25-27a, Isaac establishes sonship three times through his words. Remember—blessing, as it is used in biblical language literally means *to identify*—this is one of its definitions. So, Isaac three times sets forth sonship through his words *my son*. He identifies Jacob as his own, as having *come from* him: Isaac's bloodline and DNA.

Webster's Dictionary describes *identity* as coming from a Latin word *identidem,* which was expressed in the phrase *idem et idem*, or literally, same and same.

Genesis 1:27-28a says, "So God created man *in his own image*, in the image of God he created him; male and female he created them. God blessed them…"

The blessing sets forth ownership, establishes bloodline and identity. In the same way Isaac established this with Jacob (*my son*), God establishes with us through saying, "I created you in *My* image—you are my son, you are my daughter—you're *Mine*! You came from *Me*. I thought you up! I created you. I planned you on purpose and with purpose!" What a great position of privilege we are born into when we come into relationship with God! We literally inherit the favor, rights and privileges of a blood-born child.

Image

Not only did Isaac address the issue of his son's identity, but he also took time to speak to him regarding his individualism, or image:

So he went to him and kissed him. *When Isaac caught the smell of his clothes*, he blessed him and said, "Ah, *the smell of my son* is like the smell of a field that the LORD has blessed".

–GENESIS 27:27

Have you ever talked to someone who has recently lost a spouse or loved one? I've heard many say the thing that makes them feel the closest to their lost loved one is to take an article of their clothing and hold it up to their face and breathe in – because it still smells like them.

The sense of smell is a powerful thing. I remember opening up my crate that I had shipped from the United States to Thailand after arriving there for my first term serving as a missionary. There I stood in my little one-room rental surrounded by all of the smells of an unknown land and the sounds of a strange language I could not understand. But when I opened the crate—wow—it was like being at home again! I could smell the fragrance of my favorite candles that had been in my living room in the States. I could smell the fragrance of my favorite laundry detergent in my clothes and towels. I remember grabbing the sheets and quickly making my bed so I could crawl in and pull the sheets over my head and feel a little closer to home.

When Isaac, the daddy, caught the smell of his boy's clothes, he recalled all of the reasons why he loved and adored who his son was! In that moment, Isaac remembered all of the distinguishing characteristics that made Esau who he was—and he *blessed* him in those things. He affirmed his son's gifting, his personality and his passion as an outdoorsman. He likened his son to an open field that the Lord had blessed. He was speaking to and affirming his son's image.

This particular part of Isaac's blessing was and is so precious to me. I grew up with two older brothers and a dad, all of whom adored the outdoors. Did I even have a chance not to as well? I *loved* being outside. I loved fishing with my grandpa and my dad and brothers. I loved horses. I dreamed of the producers of *The Rifleman* TV show writing me into the script as the Rifleman's daughter, so I, too, could have my own horse like his son Mark did! And, it probably helped that I had a childhood crush on the actor who played the Rifleman. Yes, I was hopelessly an outdoors kind of girl. I was outside every day with my brothers and their neighborhood friends playing ball. I loved sports. I excelled in athletics. I had a passion for basketball. But, as a little girl, I almost felt ashamed of my passion for these things. I had a grandmother who didn't like that I wanted to be outside. One family member would often tease me and call me Ronnie instead of Renay, because of my preference to be outside playing 'like the boys'.

But then I remember a letter my mother wrote to me upon my graduation from college. I still have that letter. In it, she blessed me for my love of the outdoors, for my athletic abilities — even though she enjoyed different things, like sewing, she still valued those characteristics that she saw in me. She wisely and, I believe, under inspiration of the Holy Spirit, placed those abilities, talents and gifting into a prophetic perspective. She told me she loved those things about me, and that she could see that God had made me exactly who I am because He knew I would one day walk on foreign soil, possibly in hard places, in order to fulfill a call to missions on my life. She reminded me that the physical strength or agility He had given me would one day provide strength to carry me to those foreign lands, and to endure the challenges that awaited me there. And, let me tell you, the psychological and physical stress of the lifestyle of a missionary is, at times, grueling. My mom was speaking *the blessing* over my life. She was affirming the things I had almost come to despise because of the disdain with which they were often met. She put my characteristics, my person, my gifting, into a God-shaped perspective and gave me a glimpse of the future, leaving me with a hunger to fulfill those things for which I had been born and shaped to do. In essence she, like Isaac to Jacob, said, "I **love** those things about you—you desire those things because your Father God made you that way for His purposes in your life!" Those words freed me to see myself in a different light.

When Isaac caught the fragrance of his son, he responded by blessing and affirming him! In the same way, your Heavenly Father delights over you! Zephaniah 3:17 says, "The LORD your God is with you, He is mighty to save. He will take *great delight* in you, he will quiet you with his love, he will *rejoice over you* with singing."

When you understand the blessing of the Father over your life, it will literally quiet you—He will quiet you in your insecurities; He will show His delight for you! It will settle you in *who* you are. You are *exactly* what He planned for—even your likes and your passions!

So, we see that the blessing brings an affirmation and establishing of identity and image. The final thing that we see in the blessing given by Isaac to Jacob is the blessing for *increase*.

Increase

May God give you of heaven's dew and of earth's richness— an abundance of grain and new wine. May nations serve you and peoples bow down to you. Be lord over your brothers, and may the sons of your mother bow down to you. May those who curse you be cursed and those who bless you be blessed.

–GENESIS 27:28-29

In these two verses, Isaac was making provision for his son's future. He was activating *favor* over his life. He was calling forth provision for his material needs (vs. 27), but there was also a widening of the vision of his future as Isaac continues speaking in verse 28. I say a *widening* of the vision because of one word used in that passage: may. *May* is an old English word that means *to have power, to have the ability (am able), to be free to.* He was activating the capacity *for* increase. He was literally blessing him *to be able to and to be free to* receive and fulfill *greater* things.

I cannot count the times that my team and I have listened to people, both young and old, recounting the words of a father or mother binding them to inability. When a young boy or girl dreams a dream bigger than the shantytown in which they were raised, the mother or father quickly incapacitates them from their future by tying them to the limits within which they themselves had to live. How powerful those statements become. I have sat and listened to countless elderly people who, with tears rolling down their faces, tell of the day in which their dreams died or the day in which they turned around emotionally and spiritually and returned to their small place of limits, returning to the field of the *why it can't happen* — all because of words that killed their childlike faith to dream and their pure belief that God had a purpose and greater things for their life.

The blessing of the father could have changed all of that! Not receiving the blessing from our fathers is something the majority of our generation is dealing with. Why do we crave it so much from our natural fathers and mothers? I think it is because there is a spiritual law at work. God gave fathers the authority to set things in order in their families. God gave parents authority to bless, shape and set the course of their children's lives. But if a parent is not in right relationship with God or if they are living with soul wounds that have kept them from understanding *their* God-given position and purposes, they don't have the capacity to give what they do not have or what they do not understand. John 8:32 explains this principle: understanding truth brings freedom. Therefore, a lack of understanding or truth breeds a cycle of limitations and defeat. Understanding and declaring God's favor and plan over a child's life is like clearing a path for them to more easily access their future!

Isaac boldly peers into the future by the Spirit of the Lord and starts augmenting the future of his son. He was blessing his son with the capacity for increase—to have the good character and stewardship required of the greater things God had in store for him.

Isaac's blessing to his son addressed identity, image and the capacity for increase. What a gift! If you have never received that kind of spoken blessing from a spiritual authority in your life, you are probably at this moment saying, "Me too, Father! Bless me, too!" Just like Esau cried out!

Esau's Blessing

So, what about Esau?

Ah, Esau. He's the guy we almost feel sorry for as we read

his reaction to the situation. We're not reading of an adolescent child's reaction to losing out on some random sibling rivalry. We're reading about an adult man, who, in realizing the gravity of what he's lost, is absolutely broken. We see his insistence to his father to also bless him.

When I first felt the Lord walking me through this passage of Scripture, my focus fell to Jacob and to the words of Isaac. But as I meditated more and more, and as the Holy Spirit seemed to draw me back again and again to this story, I began to take notice of Esau.

One day when Esau was younger, he came in from a long hard day in the fields hunting. He was hungry. But, not just hungry, he was, as we sometimes put it, *starving*. How many times have we said that? "I'm *starving*!" Well, that day, Esau was *starving*.

His brother, Jacob, wasn't the outdoorsman that Esau was. He worked closer to camp. When Esau arrived, Jacob was cooking a stew. The smell of that stew was drifting through the whole camp. Esau, naturally, was drawn to it because, remember: he was starving. Being a desperate man, he asked his brother for a bowl of stew.

Now Jacob, from the womb, had been grasping for the position of the firstborn, which belonged to Esau. Because of that inner competition, he saw this as an opportunity and began bartering with Esau for Esau's birthright: his birthright in exchange for a bowl of stew.

The birthright, to simplify it, was basically the material inheritance of the firstborn son. The birthright meant that, at the time of the father's death, if there were two sons, the estate of the father would be divided not by two, but three. An extra portion was configured into the division of the estate.

That extra portion, instead of going to another heir, was the birthright of the firstborn. In this case, Esau was to be the heir of two thirds of his father's wealth, and Jacob would receive a third.

So, Jacob bartered masterfully! He took advantage of his brother's "I'm starving!" and went in for the payoff. Esau finally relented and flippantly says, "OK, take it!" Jacob, though, to insure the payoff, makes his brother swear by oath that the birthright will be his. Esau swore to it. And the Bible says in Genesis 25:34, "So Esau despised his birthright." Esau did not value his birthright and bartered it for a bowl of stew.

I imagine that as the years went by, Esau matured and recognized his mistake. He had willfully squandered off something not only of great value, but of great esteem. I think he recognized his failure and resolved not to repeat the same mistake again. So, in his natural resolve, he determined that regardless of anything else, he would not allow himself to lose out on the most coveted gift of all, which was the blessing of his father as the firstborn.

So, when the day came, and his father called him into his tent to ask him to prepare himself to receive his blessing, Esau was determined to fulfill his father's every request. He listened as his feeble, blind father began to talk to him about the special moment that he'd anticipated for so long. His father wanted the ceremonious moment to include things that were intimate between his son and himself. Like Isaac's love for the type of game meat that Esau often brought home for the family meals. So, Isaac asked him to hunt and kill the meat that would be used in their blessing meal together. He also asked Esau prepare the meal himself in the way that Isaac loved. He was then to present it to his father so that he could eat it and, afterwards, Isaac would give him the blessing.

Esau, probably reflecting on the lost birthright, left his father's room with his heart pounding and with a strength and resolve to do everything that had been asked of him without delay. This time he was going to get it right.

Meanwhile, his mom had overheard the conversation and had gone directly to Jacob to discuss it with him. When you read the story, the Bible is very clear of the favoritism that existed between each parent and both sons. Jacob was his mom's favorite, and Esau was his father's favorite. Also a driving factor in Rebekah's behavior was the prophecy that had been spoken to her by the Lord during her pregnancy: "The older (son) will serve the younger (son)." She quickly devised a plan with Jacob to deceive Isaac into speaking the blessing of the firstborn over Jacob rather than Esau. The plan was foolproof. She even took into account Isaac's blindness—age had left him without sight. Given this, she prepared animal pelts to be placed on the backs of Jacob's hands and neck, so in the event that his father might touch him, he would think it was Esau, because Esau was a hairy man. And, can I just say here — if it required animal pelts in order to pass Jacob off as Esau—Esau was apparently *really* hairy.

The plan worked like a charm. Jacob left his father's presence with the coveted blessing.

So, we pick up the story in Genesis 27:30-31,

After Isaac finished blessing him and Jacob had scarcely left his father's presence, his brother Esau came in from hunting. He too prepared some tasty food and brought it to his father. Then he said to him, "My father, sit up and eat some of my game, so that you may give me your blessing."

I can imagine his anticipation—almost his elation at having got it right! "I'm here, Dad! I did everything that you asked me to—carried it out to the last letter! Sit up, Dad! Here's the stew you asked me to make. I made it just like you always like it. Let's have some of this together and then you can give me your blessing!"

But, instead, his father Isaac asked him, "Who are you?"

You have to think that something in his heart sank at that question, "Who are you?" He responds strongly and declares his position as firstborn.

"I am your son," he answered, "your firstborn, Esau."
Isaac trembled violently and said, "Who was it, then, that hunted game and brought it to me? I ate it just before you came and I blessed him—and indeed he will be blessed!"

—Genesis 27:32-33

Isaac had sensed something was off when Jacob had entered into his quarters. He asked him, "Are you sure you're Esau, my firstborn?" Instead of relying on what he sensed in his heart, he relied on what he felt with his hands and what he identified as the smell of Esau's clothes. Imagine the regret he must've had at this eye-opening moment!

Remember what I said about the blessing? Even if it were given in error, it couldn't be retracted! Thus we see the response of Isaac, "I blessed him—and indeed he will be blessed!"

When Esau heard his father's words, he burst out with a

loud and bitter cry and said to his father, "Bless me—me too, my father!"

"No, Dad, please! This time I did it right! I did everything in my power to obey, to be good, to please you, to measure up! Please—bless me! Bless me, too, my Father!"

In verses 35-37 of the same chapter, we see the interaction between father and son play out:

> But he said, "Your brother came deceitfully and took your blessing." Esau said, "Isn't he rightly named Jacob? He has deceived me these two times: He took my birthright, and now he's taken my blessing!" Then he asked, "Haven't you reserved any blessing for me?"
>
> What great loss, what great displacement Esau must have felt in that very moment.
>
> Isaac answered Esau, "I have made him lord over you and have made all his relatives his servants, and I have sustained him with grain and new wine. So what can I possibly do for you, my son?"

How many of us have had a moment like this? This was a life-defining moment. Something happened in the workings of Esau's soul right here in this moment. He knew he had squandered off his birthright the first time, sure. But this time he realized that even though he'd done everything in his power to make life work for him, someone else came in and stole his future out from under him. Something happened to him that was truly out of his control. He was left penniless, so to speak. His future was stripped from him, and he was robbed of everything that he had hoped for. He was heartbroken. But even in his heartbrokenness, he held out for something, anything from his father. One version of this next Scripture says that Esau insisted.

> Esau said to his father, "Do you have only one blessing, my father? Bless me too, my Father!" Then Esau wept aloud.
>
> —GENESIS 27:38

This next part is the part where most of us stop reading this story. Why? Because it sounds so depressing, it sounds like some kind of sad consolation prize. But keep reading —I'll meet you at the end of this part!

> His father Isaac answered him, "Your dwelling will be away from the earth's richness, away from the dew of heaven above. "You will live by the sword and you will serve your brother. But when you grow restless, you will throw his yoke from off your neck"
>
> —GENESIS 27:39-40

Hebrews 11:20 puts the above-mentioned Scripture in perspective. Yeah, I know. It's the faith chapter. So what in the world does it have to do with Esau? Look at what verse 20 says: "By faith Isaac *blessed* Jacob *and Esau* in regard to their future".

If you're like me, you're probably saying, "Wait. Hold up! That is a blessing? Where, exactly, is the blessing in what Isaac spoke to his son Esau in Genesis 27:39-40?" My feelings exactly — until I finally saw it. It's at the end of verse 40: *"But* when you grow restless, *you will throw his yoke from off your neck"* (Gen. 27:39-40).

That word *but* either works *in* your favor or *against* it. This time, it fell in Esau's favor. Isaac repeated the parts of the blessing he had activated in the life of Jacob—the parts that would also affect Esau in relationship with Jacob—which, I'm *sure* was pure bitterness for Esau to hear!

Then he says, "But." But — *when you grow restless*, you will *throw his yoke from off your neck*. What a statement!

A yoke is defined as a wooden bar used to attach the head or neck of one animal to the head or neck of another animal or to the driver of a plow. It's also described as being something that embraces two parts to hold or unite them in position.

When we suffer an injustice, such as Esau suffered, or perhaps like you suffered through childhood sexual abuse, through emotional or physical abandonment or violence, the enemy's plan is to immediately lower that wooden bar over your neck in order to attach you to that moment for life. An injustice or soul wound left unresolved can literally transform itself into a yoke that unites you *in position* with that person, experience or situation.

When I lived in Southeast Asia, it was commonplace to see water buffalo working in the rice fields. In places like Cambodia and Thailand, modern tractors are practically unheard of. But the good ole water buffalo are still out there plowing away. When the driver of the plow places the yoke over the neck and head of an animal, that animal no longer has the freedom to move about freely. He is yoked to the will and whim of the driver. Its world is reduced to that singular plot of land. When that ox is driven to the border of the field, the driver manipulates the yoke to turn the animal around and cycle it back down another row again and again. That animal's purpose and boundaries have been determined for him by that yoke.

Esau came under a yoke. It would affect him emotionally

and spiritually. It would drive him to a murderous rage. His father recognized that the yoke had been lowered over his son's neck. Even though his father did not have the power to undo the injustice, he gave him a blessing that would supersede it (supercede means to force out something as being inferior; to displace in favor of another).

I want to paraphrase the story here. Here's what was happening: Isaac truly *was* speaking a blessing over the life of Esau. He was saying, "Son, for a while you are going to live under this yoke of anger and rage from the injustice of your brother. I cannot take back the words that I spoke over his life, nor can I deactivate what has been set into motion prophetically. But son, there is something that I *can* do! I have the God-given authority to activate something over your life and your future! And, Son, today, I prophecy a *day* in the calendar of your future. It's going to start out like any other day—but rest assured, it will be different. You'll get up as usual. But on that day, Son, you're going to get up and realize the weariness of living and relating your life and your person through that yoke of injustice. You're going to be ready to be rid of that heavy yoke once and for all. And, Son, when that moment hits you, *I bless you with an anointing, a divine resolve and supernatural grace and strength to cast that thing off of your neck!* I bless you to *come out from under what marked you, what limited you, what incapacitated you! On that day, you will be free!*"

What a blessing! What grace! This is what our heavenly Father did for us through our adoption as children through the blood of the Lord Jesus Christ! He blessed us so we could come *out from under* a yoke of injustice, sin and bondage, and so we could take on a brand new identity and image in Jesus! He blessed us so we would have the capacity for increase, for going from glory to glory. I'm not saying that the whole journey will be glorious, but I'm saying everything in the journey will only serve to strengthen and mold and guide us toward all He purposed for us to be and accomplish through Him! He has blessed us with supernatural grace and deliverance so that the injustices, the unspeakable horrors so many have suffered need not define who we are nor set limits in regard to our future!

Jesus said,

> Come to me, all you who are weary and burdened, and I will give you rest. Take my yoke upon you and learn from me, for I am gentle and humble in heart, and you will find rest for your souls. For my yoke is easy and my burden is light.
> —MATTHEW 11:28-30

In Christ, our Father God frees us from a yoke of slavery and offers us a yoke of freedom, friendship and peace with God. The injustices, trauma, or failures of your life are not the determining factors for your future, friend. There's something that supersedes all of that: it's the blessing of your Father. You have His favor and unconditional love. May you feel supernatural strength to throw that yoke from off of your neck—and to move forward to something greater!

CHAPTER 3

SPIRITUAL WARFARE 101

"In spiritual warfare, it's not a question of power, but position!"

I know this sounds so weird, but I actually like to watch boxing! It makes me laugh just saying that I like boxing! It's such a guy sport, but I really get into it when I happen to catch a boxing match on TV.

Boxing is interesting (ok, you may not think so, but stay with me!). Or, maybe I should say, it has interesting principles. Strength is definitely important. Conditioning is paramount. But, with boxing, the biggest man isn't always the one guaranteed to win. Size does not guarantee a championship. In boxing, the winner isn't always the one who appears stronger. In fact, sometimes it's the short guy who wins, or the skinny guy, or the one, who, for some other reason, simply appears less capable of winning.

So how does he win?

He wins by understanding how to *position* himself. He knows how and when to move. He knows how to position his feet. A champion understands that correct positioning will open the door for him to take his opponent down.

In spiritual warfare, it works the same way. Victory isn't a question of power, but of position!

Before I jump into talking about our spiritual position and authority, I have to confess something: I used to be a spiritual warfare skeptic. I believed in the general idea of spiritual warfare, but the extremes in doctrine (and in the lingo associated with it) made me want to avoid the subject altogether.

I continued with my platonic approach to the subject until I began to experience spiritual attacks both personally and in my ministry. I came to a point where I could no longer deny that the enemy was, without a doubt, fighting against me and against the efforts of our ministry team. Talk about some huge reality checks!

This was when I began to ask the Holy Spirit to school me in spiritual warfare. I asked the Lord to reveal truth to me from His Word regarding the reality of the spirit realm. I wanted to know *why* I believed what I believed, and I wanted to understand why I prayed the way I prayed when coming against the enemy. I needed to be certain of my own position regarding biblical strategies for engaging the enemy and effecting real change.

One day I had a heart to heart talk with my good friend, Graciela, about the subject of spiritual warfare. I asked a lot of questions. Remember, I had heard and read a lot on the subject over the years. But God was trying to give me more than just knowledge—He was trying to equip me with *revelation knowledge,* which is knowledge with understanding and conviction (being convinced!).

Graciela and I often travel and minister together, so, consequently, we often pray together. When praying together before a service, many times we came against the enemy using phrases such as, "We bind you," "I come against a spirit of," "we resist you," "we rebuke you," "we renounce this or that," "we loose that person." I confess—I was struggling with skepticism—even while praying those things (and I'd prayed them for years!). Even though my mind believed, my heart was grappling with the integrity of those kinds of prayers. Were they prayers or formulas? Were we being effective or emotional?

Soon after my talk with Graciela, we were scheduled to minister together at a women's conference in the United States. To accommodate the large group of women registered, it was scheduled for two consecutive weekends. In light of our conversation about spiritual warfare, we began to pray that the Lord would give us a demonstration in the natural of what we were really up against in the spirit realm. Simply put—we wanted evidence that what we were doing was spiritually effective.

As I prepared for the conference, the Holy Spirit gave me a fresh Word to minister. I felt so strongly about the message that I'd prepared. For me, it was fresh revelation on confronting generational strongholds. If there were ever a topic having to do with demonic strongholds and spiritual warfare, it was this topic!

As I stepped into the pulpit the second evening of the

conference, and opened my Bible, I felt like a million bucks! I was excited about delivering this new message. Little did I know what would happen in the following moments!

As I began to read the very first verse of Scripture, suddenly I felt deathly ill. If anyone would have asked me, "Where does it hurt?" I would not have been able to give an answer. I felt sick from head to toe. I think even my *hair* hurt! In addition to that, I could not focus or think. I couldn't seem to get anything intelligible to come out of my mouth. A sentence would form in my mouth and then my mind would go absolutely blank.

You might say, "Well, that happens to all of us every once in a while." Yes, but I'm talking about *every single sentence*!

Then, I began to have crazy thoughts like, *You are never going to make it through this sermon—and not only that, you will never make it to the end of your ministry. You are going to die.* I was finding it hard to stand up. My hair was soaked within 10 minutes because I began to sweat profusely (lovely, right?). I knew that the only way to make it through my message was to *read* my notes straight through. So, that's what I did! I gripped the pulpit so hard my knuckles turned white as I read the words I believed the Holy Spirit gave me for those ladies. I'm sure they thought that my style of preaching was…unique. They had no idea what was really happening.

As I finished my notes, a holy anger rose up within me. I felt the authority of Jesus Christ! A fight rose up inside of me! Stepping to the side of the pulpit, gripping it with one hand and the microphone with the other, I said, "In the name of the Lord Jesus, I bind you foul spirits that have bound these ladies and their families for generations. I take dominion over you right now in the name of the Lord Jesus Christ: Loose these ladies!"

Oh my goodness. It was as if I'd tossed a bomb out into the crowd! Immediately, there were multiple demonic manifestations. One woman had run to the front before I even gave the altar call. When I took authority over the strongholds, she immediately crashed to the ground right in front of me.

This took place in a matter of seconds. Though my eyes were seeing everything, my mind continued telling me, '*Hey—remember, you're dying*'. I still felt deathly ill. I came down off the stage, walked straight over to the director of the event, and said, "Here."—handing her the microphone! She stared at me with a shocked look on her face, like, *Really?* I created a disaster and then handed off the microphone to her! I looked at Graciela and said, "Gra, I'm so sick." She looked at me with a panicked expression and told me to go to my cabin, and she would follow me and bring my things.

Somehow, I managed to get to my cabin. I walked in and fell onto the bed. Moments later Graciela entered, took one look at me, and said, "This is demonic!" Ah, how we laugh at that now! At the time, I was thinking, *Duh! You think!?* I remember vividly looking up at her and saying, "Gra, I feel this, this, this and this" (naming off four things). She laid hands on me and took authority over the enemy. I agreed in prayer like I'd never agreed in prayer before!

After she prayed, she said, "I have to get back to the service—God is moving in a powerful way! People are being set free right and left!"

I said, "Yes, go! I'll be fine." After she prayed over me and throughout the course of the night, I finally began to recover.

The next day, I was to minister the closing service of the conference. I awoke like a different person! It was as if nothing had happened. I went to the service, stepped up behind the pulpit, and the Holy Spirit came down! Before I even preached, there were scores of people baptized in the Holy Spirit for the first time. Many people were physically healed. I preached my heart out, felt a God-given flow in the language (I was preaching in Spanish), and overall, it was a great morning!

Afterwards, Graciela and I made our way back to our book and resource table.

A line of ladies had formed to greet us personally before making their purchases and leaving the conference. One lady in particular approached me wanting to talk. I told her we could sit down and chat once I had finished greeting the others. She waited.

Finally, while things were coming to a close and the musicians were hauling their equipment to the bus, I sat down with her. I'm not sure how else to explain what I felt except that I felt she was acting mystical, and it agitated me. She looked at me and said, "I owe you an apology."

I said, "How could you owe me an apology? We don't know each other."

She replied, "Oh, but I *do* owe you an apology. What happened to you last night—I did that."

She *immediately* had my attention, since no one else knew of my sickness besides Graciela and the leadership. The hair on the back of my neck stood up. I said, "Uh-huh, uhm, give me just one second." I stood up and said, "GRACIELA! Come here!" I was calling for back up! We sat and intently listened to this lady's story.

She was a Satanist and had lived in bondage since making a covenant with Satan a few years earlier. She began to tell me, "Last night, when they were calling you to the platform, Satan told me to go outside. He guided me to two cabins where I worked magic over a black rock. Then I buried the rock in the ground between the two cabins. He then told me to return to the service where I was to curse you with four things as you were preaching."

Friend—the four things that she named were the exact symptoms or thoughts that I had told Graciela I was fighting the previous night when she came into my cabin to pray for me! And by the way, those two cabins where this lady said Satan instructed her to bury the black rock? Graciela's and mine.

God was answering our prayers. He had allowed us to see a demonstration in the natural realm of what was really happening in the spirit realm as we ministered. He showed us the law of 'cause and effect' in a spiritual context. Through this experience, God taught me that even our physical bodies and minds could suffer attacks from the enemy. Without spiritual discernment, such attacks could easily be relegated as mere happenstance.

The gifts of the Spirit are critical elements needed to successfully navigate spiritual warfare as we experience it in our daily walk with God and our ministry to others. The discerning of spirits, in particular, is one of the gifts of the Spirit that is often forgotten. This particular Holy Spirit gift is especially valuable in helping us identify the source behind frustration, an impasse in ministry, or a lack of breakthrough—whether it be in your general ministry, or, in a particular church service or outreach (such as what I went through at the conference).

Developing a dependency on the gifts of the Spirit will save you time and energy in spiritual battles.

Let me tell you the rest of the story. Graciela and I returned the following weekend to the same campground and conference center to minister to another group of ladies. This time, however, we felt better prepared for what might await us.

After the first night of ministry, we returned to our respective cabins. We still had the keys from the previous weekend and supposedly no one had access to our cabins during the week. The next morning, I went to Graciela's cabin for coffee before the morning service. As I approached her cabin, she threw the door open, catching me by surprise. She exclaimed, "Friend—look!" and pointed to a pile of black sand and acorns on the floor by the door.

I laughed and said, "Have you started a new hobby of acorn collecting?"

She said, "No. Last night when I pulled back the cover of my bed, there was a work of black magic ritually placed across the sheet and under my pillows. It gave me chills! I immediately swept it off the bed, and began to take dominion over any work of witchcraft, magic, etc. I was determined not to be intimidated, so I got into bed to go to sleep."

"And, were you able to sleep?" I asked.

"Not at all!" she exclaimed. We chuckled and looked at each other knowingly. *Here we go again!* I decided right then and there to spend the afternoon in my cabin praying and fasting for the evening service.

Remember the illustration of the boxing match? In spiritual warfare, it's not a question of power, but of position! We cannot compete with the power of the enemy—that's not our job anyway! Paul writes in I Corinthians 2:4, "My message and my preaching were not with wise and persuasive words, but with a demonstration of the *Spirit's* power!" And listen to what Zechariah 4:6 says: "Not by might, nor by power, but by my Spirit says the Lord of hosts!" We needed the Lord of hosts (the Lord who has an army, a hierarchy of angels) to show up and restrain the enemy...and cast him out! Once the enemy was exposed to us we understood that the game was *on*. We immediately took action by prayer, fasting, and in listening to the Spirit all day in preparation. We knew that *positionally* we had authority over the enemy's power.

That same night, I again stood before the women attending and delivered the same message on confronting generational strongholds. I was prepared—I had saturated myself, as well as the service in prayer. At one point, the Holy Spirit gave me a word of knowledge (a revealing of something not previously known in the natural) that there were many there who had in their possession trinkets and things associated with ancestral worship or occultism. Friend, this wasn't the 18th century—this was 2010! We weren't deep in a jungle in some remote foreign land—we were in the United States! Through the gift of the Spirit I called those things out. I instructed the ladies to run to their dorms and cabins and to bring those items back to the auditorium. About a dozen ran out—some were teenagers, some were grandmothers. It was uncanny what happened next. As each one brought those things forward, dropping them at the altar area, deliverance began! There were some very strong demonic manifestations—many became physically ill. But what happened next was one of the most powerful things that I have ever witnessed. When people began to confront the strongholds and renounce them—when they brought symbols and trinkets that were attached to childhood ceremonies, astrology or activities of spiritism, the Holy Spirit came through that place like a wave! First we spent nearly two hours praying for deliverance—and then a powerful move of the Holy Spirit swept through with salvations, spontaneous baptisms in the Holy Spirit, physical healings, forgiveness, and freedom from torment. Hallelujah!

Following the service, we headed back to our cabins. As Graciela opened her cabin door, I caught a glimpse of all the acorns and other things that she'd found under her covers the night before. "Gra, throw those things out of your cabin!" I exclaimed. But, exhausted, she muttered, "I'll deal with it in the morning."

Early the next day, I returned to Graciela's cabin for coffee. Again she threw open the door and said, "Friend—look!"

I looked down and saw that the acorns and trinkets were gone. I said, "Good! You finally threw them out!"

"No, I didn't," she said. Then she began to recount her night: After a tumultuous night of spiritual warfare (including something rattling the windows and doors of the cabin from front to back) she finally climbed into bed at 4:30 a.m. Unable to sleep, she got up at 6:00 a.m. When she got up, she discovered that all of the acorns and trinkets had disappeared.

We immediately prayed together—specifically binding the work of the enemy, the strongman, by using Scripture and by verbally taking dominion over him. We asked the Holy Spirit to overshadow the meddling activity of the enemy and to bring great breakthrough that day in the final service. The Holy Spirit did not disappoint. The Presence of the Lord showed up powerfully and poured out joy and freedom!

The breakthrough was amazing—but it didn't happen without a fight!

I didn't include this story to add an air of sensationalism to my book. Nor did I include it to glorify the work of the enemy or invite unnecessary fear about some kind of constant lurking threat of black magic or Satanism. My heart's desire is that this story would have the same impact on you that it did on Graciela and me. Consider it a wake-up call, a reality check. I hope you will see it as an affirmation of the authority that God has given you to pull down strongholds.

This experience gave me such confidence, assurance and *faith* in God's Word! It changed my prayer life! It demonstrated to me that we are not just crazy Christians, praying fruitless prayers and making loud but powerless declarations! We are not boxing the air!

When you pray—when you go into a place to bring light—when you stand in your family, in your community or behind whatever other pulpit God has given you—you stand with a supernatural authority commissioned by the God of heaven and earth—authority to bring freedom. The enemy will mock you in your thoughts—he'll tell you that what you are doing is silly and senseless! You'll hear the words of the secular world rolling through your mind as you pray, as you fast, as you prepare to minister. Those thoughts are the enemy's smokescreen. He will try to intimidate you so that you take an earthly posture toward your situation. But, as God spoke to countless of His servants in the Word, "Be of good courage! Fear not! I am with you!" You are not fighting alone—God Himself is backing you. When you pray—when you act—there is a *shift* that happens in the spirit! And that's why, many times, all hell breaks loose when you begin to move!

Fundamentals of Spiritual Warfare

So, let's talk about spiritual warfare. Who is it that battles or fights this fight in the spirit? Scripture identifies three entities that are directly involved in spiritual warfare. They are Jesus, angels and us.

We know that the Bible tells us in Romans 8:34 that Jesus is interceding for us constantly. He's in this fight with us. Fighting for us. Praying for us!

Secondly, we know that there are angels sent by God to fight on our behalf or on God's behalf. They are assigned.

Before I go any further, let me say this: *We should not pray to the angels!* Colossians 2:18-19 is very clear on this subject! It says,

> Do not let anyone who delights in false humility *and the worship of angels* disqualify you for the prize. Such a person goes into great detail about what he has seen, and his unspiritual mind puffs him up with idle notions. He has lost connection with the Head, from whom the whole body, supported and held together by its ligaments and sinews, grows as God causes it to grow.

Angels and all things supernatural are really trendy right now—but as Christians, we need to be very careful and discerning regarding these things, making sure our approach to them is based on Scripture.

In Daniel 10, we find a great illustration concerning the role of angels. Daniel's experience demonstrates that angels are involved in spiritual warfare, and that there exists a spiritual hierarchy, not only with God, but also within the kingdom of darkness.

God gave Daniel a vision concerning future events that

included hardship and war. The vision troubled Daniel because he didn't understand it. So he began to fast. He fasted for 21 days, continually asking God to give him understanding.

Shortly after the three-week fast was up, Daniel was out walking with friends. Suddenly, an angel appeared to him. Everyone who was with Daniel ran and hid. Only Daniel saw the appearance of the heavenly man. The angel spoke to him and eventually touched him and stood him on his feet. Then he said,

> Do not be afraid, Daniel. Since the first day that you set your mind to gain understanding and to humble yourself before your God, your words were heard, and I have come in response to them. *But the prince of the Persian kingdom resisted me twenty-one days. Then Michael, one of the chief princes, came to help me, because I was detained there with the king of Persia.* Now I have come to explain to you what will happen to your people in the future, for the vision concerns a time yet to come.
>
> —DANIEL 10:12-14

What a powerful picture! See how God responds when we seek Him through prayer and fasting? Things within the spirit realm are *activated* as a direct result of our prayer and fasting (of our engaging with, and seeking answers from God). Spiritual warfare prayer is bi-directional: Our praying *to* God engages a battle *against* the enemy. God continually draws humanity to cooperate with Him for His eternal plan, while Satan and his hierarchy continually try to undermine both God's plan and God's children.

Understanding Your Enemy

So, Jesus and angels are engaged in this spiritual war of the ages, but what about you and me? *Are we called to engage in the battle?*

I've heard a variety of responses from people regarding their opinion of spiritual warfare. Some say, "I'm not really a fighter." Others say, "That's not my ministry or my gifting". Still others prefer to ignore the enemy altogether so that they don't have to take responsibility and engage in the battle. Friend, whether we recognize it or not, we are in the throes of war.

Spiritual warfare is the conflict that is stirred up in the spirit realm when we, as individuals, move forward and advance spiritually in our relationship with the Lord. So, spiritual warfare, more than being centered around one single battle, is really about an entire war. This ongoing war of the ages, as I said before, is all about seeing God's kingdom come and His will done, here on earth even as it is in heaven! It's about the presence of Jesus and the authority of God being established here on earth. This happens via you and me. God's kingdom being established and His will being done here on earth has to do with the character and love of Jesus taking deep root and being demonstrated in our own character and daily life. Preaching and doing good works is the easy part! Living, acting and reacting with the character of Jesus is the greater challenge, but also brings a greater breakthrough!

In and of ourselves we would never be much of a threat to Satan. But, when we cooperate with the Holy Spirit, and begin to administrate the works of Christ in our everyday world, we become a viable threat to him. When we understand who the enemy is and begin to recognize the way he works (delays, roadblocks, resistance), we become less susceptible to discouragement and less apt to quickly lose confidence in what we feel God has called us to do. Don't wait for something to appear overly mystical before you consider that the enemy is on the attack. He often uses people and everyday situations to throw us off kilter. Without spiritual discernment our tendency will be to incorrectly identify our enemy as (for example) lack of funds, a difficult personality, an unwilling board or committee, etc. Yes, there have been times when I felt like my enemy had a specific name, physical address and cell phone number! But our fight is not against flesh and blood, but against principalities and powers, the world-rulers of this darkness and against the spiritual hosts of wickedness in the heavenly realm (Eph. 6:12). Spiritual discernment will keep you focused and steady.

Push Back the Darkness!

So, does the average Christian really make a difference in this universal spiritual war? I love what Dean Sherman says in his book, *Spiritual Warfare For Every Christian*. He says, "The devil is equally threatened and equally defeated by each and every Christian who stands in Christ's victory and consistently practices the principles of spiritual warfare. We were meant to be actively destroying those things that would hinder or corrupt the Kingdom of God, pushing back the powers of darkness."

Push back the darkness! Are we to strong-arm the enemy in order to push him out? No. Natural power cannot drive out spiritual power. Only spiritual authority can drive out spiritual power. You might have questioned if you really do have spiritual authority. You might be questioning this even more fervently if you feel that you haven't seen any sign of break-through in your situation.

Let me give you a couple of Scriptures that speak the tremendous spiritual authority you have.

The first one is found in Acts 17:26. "From one man he made all the nations, that they should inhabit the whole earth; and he marked out their appointed times in history and the boundaries of their lands."

I love this Scripture. This is powerful! God is telling us that He marked out our appointed time in history, and that he assigned us territory in which we should live *and have dominion*! There is nothing coincidental about where you are, nor about the time in history in which you live. We are participating in a multi-generational plan! And, let there be no doubt: There is a God-given mandate and anointing upon us. And we have God-given spiritual authority that enables us to carry out and fulfill God's plans for our generation!

Remember the words Mordecai spoke to Esther centuries ago: And who knows but that you have come to your royal position *for such a time as this*? You have literally been *positioned with authority* for this time, for the place you are at, or the place God has called you to.

So, you have a God-given mandate to be where you are! God has selected your times. There is a greater mandate on your life and your days than you might have imagined until now.

Colossians 1 assures us that there is a very real kingdom of darkness; a kingdom that has dominion when it finds legal spiritual loopholes giving it entrance. Sin is a loophole for the enemy. It gives him legal rights to enter. Colossians 1 says that when we began a relationship with God through the sacrifice of Jesus for our sins, we were literally rescued out from the dominion of darkness. In other words, we had a domain change.

According to Acts 17:26, we were *created* to reign and to administrate the Kingdom of God in the territory where He has placed us in order to displace and push back the darkness.

Romans 5:17 says it so clearly, "For if *by one man's offence death reigned by one*; much more they which receive abundance of grace and of the gift of righteousness *shall reign in life by one, Jesus Christ.*"

May God shatter the "survivor" mentality in our generation! We aren't called to survive—we are called to reign! Sin allowed the enemy to have dominion over our lives and territory, but grace and the gift of right standing with God was birthed through Jesus, giving us spiritual authority over sin and over the curse of the enemy.

So, how can we conquer our fear of the giants occupying our territory? We have to remember: Our fight is spiritual, not physical. Like in the boxing analogy, neither size nor power dictates victory—position does! You're probably thinking, *Yeah, well, that's easy for you to say! You've never seen the giants that I'm staring at right now!*

Listen, Satan is nothing more than a usurper. Satan has usurped man's dominion in the earth! He has simply taken up position where we've refused. Adam and his descendents were to have dominion in the earth. But, sin was the loophole by which Satan gained legal access to oppress and deceive, to bully and badger, steal and destroy, until the authority of God is administered—putting a stop to his freedom! *Administrating the authority of Christ establishes the enemy's boundaries.*

So the truth about our giants is this: They have limits.

Satan himself is a created being with limits. When he was cast out of heaven, God established boundaries on his activity.

Let's go back to Colossians 1:15-20:

"The Son is the image of the invisible God, the firstborn over all creation. For in him all things were created: things in heaven and on earth, visible and invisible, whether thrones or powers or rulers or authorities; all things have been created through him and for him. He is before all things, and in him all things hold together. And he is the head of the body, the church; he is the beginning and the firstborn from among the dead, so that in everything he might have the supremacy. For God was pleased to have all his fullness dwell in him, and through him to reconcile to himself all things, whether things on earth or things in heaven, by making peace through his blood, shed on the cross."

All things were created by Him and for Him! He created all things visible, invisible, all powers and rulers, including all of the giants that are threatening you and occupying the territory God assigned to you as an inheritance. Those giants enjoy the freedom to operate and dominate until someone steps in and challenges their right to that land. When someone steps in and applies the authority of Christ, the trespasser's boundaries are immediately set in order. Authority sets the boundaries or the limits of power. ***Authority trumps power!*** The power of the enemy cannot advance further than the authority of God allows. Authority applied displaces power.

Colossians 1:15-20 talks about the supremacy of Christ in both the visible and invisible realm. It also speaks of the heavenly realm (or heavenly places—as also seen in Dan. 10, Eph. 6:12, and Eph. 2:6). When translated from the original, the phrase "heavenly realm" not only refers to heaven, or, the dwelling place of God and angels, but also refers to the air, the atmosphere, the invisible realm, or the realm where the kingdom of darkness wages war. Spiritual battles, then, are not solely internal conflicts within an individual, but are external as well.

As mentioned previously, there exists an entire hierarchy in the kingdom of darkness, which includes demons, principalities and powers. Demons can be cast out (of individuals), but principalities and powers (for instance, the regional Prince of Persia assigned to a specific territory in Daniel 10) must be displaced. Someone has to push that principality out! How? Enter into that territory and occupy! Presence!

According to Colossians 1, God has called you to reconcile territory unto Him! His goal is that all things would be reconciled unto Himself, whether things on earth or things in heaven (which is to say, in the heavenly realm).

The word *reconcile* means to restore to harmony. It also means to settle, to resolve (as in, resolve conflicts or differences), and to cause to submit to or accept something unpleasant.

When God stirs us to cross a border and take new territory spiritually, that is certainly unpleasant to the enemy! He absolutely 100 percent opposes your advancement! Why? Because *you* represent the presence of the Lord Jesus in the earth in this generation! And when you raise your foot up and place it down in territory where he has dominated illegally, he will unleash the power of hell on you in order to drive you back! Why? Because the enemy and his imps do not want to submit to Christ! And they know that their power is not legally binding over the authority of Jesus, which operates through you and through me.

We must understand, when we confront the enemy, that we enter into the ring with an advantage. We might not look tough. We might not be as big as him. We might be mocked because our weapons of prayer and fasting and submission to the Holy Spirit might appear as little rocks in our hands compared to size and strength of the giant. But, we're not fighting a fight of power. We're fighting a fight of spiritual rights and authority! We're pushing against the darkness by occupying our position spiritually. Jesus, who reconciled us — restored harmony to our soul, settled us spiritually, resolved our conflict with sin and caused us to submit wholeheartedly to Him —has also given us the *ministry* of reconciliation (2 Cor. 5:18). Our generational assignment, then, is to administrate the Kingdom and reign with Christ's authority over the powers of darkness in the places where God has set us. Part of our spiritual inheritance as co-heirs with Christ is to restore harmony where sin has caused conflict and devastation. So, when you step into the ring, remember—your God-given authority trumps the power of your giant, and *he must submit* to the Word of the Lord and to the Lord's servant!

You Are Already Positioned

Finally, let me wrap this chapter up with a truth that revolutionized my spiritual life with regard to intercession and spiritual warfare.

One of the most quoted passages of the Bible about spiritual warfare is Ephesians 6:10-13. Take a look at the passage here, and notice the emphasis I've added:

"*Finally,* be strong in the Lord and in his mighty power. Put on the full armor of God, so that you can take your stand against the devil's schemes. For our struggle is not against flesh and blood, but against the rulers, against the authorities, against the powers of this dark world and against the spiritual forces of evil in the heavenly realms. Therefore put on the full armor of God, so that when the day of evil comes, you may be able to stand your ground, and after you have done everything, to stand."

These verses start out with "Finally…" The verses that follow "finally" are about engaging in the battle. But before you engage, before you even put the armor on, you have to understand your ranking. "Finally" indicates prerequisites to this passage. Ephesians is all about position! The author was saying that you have to understand your position in order to stand against the enemy. It's all about who we are in Christ, and how it came about that we gained our present position (through Christ's death on the cross and our subsequent adoption as children of God, joint-heirs with Jesus).

In Ephesians, Paul lays out three critical elements in the foundation of Christian life (D. Sherman): sitting, walking, and standing. Only after emphasizing sitting and walking does he speak about being strong in the Lord and putting on the armor to engage the enemy.

With regard to sitting, Ephesians 2:6 says, "And God raised us up with Christ and *seated us with him in the heavenly realms* in Christ Jesus."

When the Lord helped me understand the implications of this verse, it blew me away! When I first started meditating and studying it, I focused on the heavenly realms part. But the key to the verse is the simple preposition *in*. This is a preposition that, in the Greek, denotes a fixed position in *time, place and state*. In other words, when we were adopted as children of God through Jesus Christ our *position* was established. It is not limited, increased or altered by time, because it is an *eternal* position. It is not limited by place because we are talking about our spirit, and the heavenly realm. Our position was eternally *established* even while we still exist in the body within the confines of earthly time.

Paul was certainly not referring to our current physical position when he said we have been seated with Christ. We are not in heaven *physically* seated with Christ. But our spirit has already been elevated to that position of authority! Primarily, we are a spirit being—our temporary housing is this physical body. But our position of being seated with Christ, as a joint-heir, reigning with Christ in authority, has been put into place, not because of where we are, but because of *who* we are!

To give a clearer perspective let me put it this way: When Jesus returns for the rapture of the Church, or if we die, when He raises us up and takes us to heaven with him, what will change regarding our body, soul, and spirit? Our bodies will be redeemed—they will be perfected and take on immortality. A lot of us could shout over that! We want a changed body—a better one! What about our soul? Our soul is our mind, our will and our emotions — the fleshly, carnal nature. Will that change when we get to heaven? Yes, the soul will be completely redeemed and perfected on that amazing day! No more struggling against temptation and sin! But, what of our spirit? Will our spirit change? No. Why? *Because our spirit has already been raised up with Christ and seated with Him in the heavenly realms*—positioned for reigning in life, for administrating the Kingdom of God, for pushing back the darkness—though our spirit is not physically seated with Christ in heaven, we have been positioned in the spirit as if we were already there with Him!

Let me be very clear that I am not saying we have been elevated to a position equal to God! But let me be equally as clear in saying that we have been delegated the authority of the Lord Jesus Christ in order to establish His Kingdom, take back territory and burst onto the scene of new territory here on earth! We have been raised up with Christ and seated with him in the heavenly realms (Eph 2:6) in order that we might reign in life (Rom. 5:17), so that His will would be accomplished here on earth (Matt. 6:10: "Thy kingdom come, Thy will be done in earth, as it is in heaven.").

You are in a battle to break from the chains of your past, and to advance and move forward to your God-given destiny. Or you are in a battle to free others from their past so that they can advance and enjoy an abundant life. That's why you are reading this book! In order to accomplish those things, you *must* be clear on your RIGHT to take back what was stolen from you by the strongman, as well as your right to move into territory that God has allotted to you as an inheritance! You must understand the authority you have to drive out trespassing giants—spiritual squatters who are occupying and refusing to budge from what God said is yours for the taking! You need the confidence that walking with Jesus brings—walking in holiness gives you courage in the face of the enemy!

When God helps you to grasp your position and the authority you have in Him, your prayer life will change! You will no longer pray, "God, I ask *You* to remove that obstacle." Or "God, I ask *you* to move and make this or that happen." Instead, you will begin to pray, "I take dominion over you foul spirits that are blocking the advancement of God's will for my life, or for that city or for that nation or for that person. And in the name of the Lord Jesus, I command you to come out of that place and to loose your hold on my territory!" It's not a matter of bravado. You aren't jumping around the boxing ring simply talking a big talk. It's a matter of being spiritually pro-active and stepping into your God-given position. It's a matter of understanding your right to take up and administrate spiritual authority, rather than asking God to do something He's already delegated you authority to accomplish! Remember: *Authority trumps power!* Go push back some darkness!

CHAPTER 4

TEN STRATEGIES FOR EFFECTIVE SPIRITUAL WARFARE

To move forward in your life, spiritual walk, and quest for re-claiming your spiritual rights, requires engaging, confronting and pushing *out* the enemy.

Previously, I talked about the hierarchy that exists in the spiritual realm. I talked about the fact that demons can be cast out, but principalities and powers have to be displaced. Dis-placing requires presence. It requires someone to move in on the enemy's territory and push him out. Then, there's the work of staying there in order to maintain that victory and new territory. This works on a corporate (Church) and individual level. I want to focus mostly on the individual. How can you, as an individual, successfully engage in spiritual warfare?

First of all, you have to recognize your need for growth in certain areas of your life, whether that area is in your character, weaknesses, or in the area of your ministry calling. You have to be able to identify areas of stagnancy or impasse in your life, both spiritually and in situations in the natural.

Second, you have to believe it is God's desire for you to extend your territory. You have to truly know in your heart that it is His will for you to increase (be blessed) and advance in the spirit, in life, and in ministry. You have to believe wholeheartedly in the fact that there are greater things yet to come—things that have been assigned to your life by God.

Dean Sherman, in his book *Spiritual Warfare For Every Christian,* says, "The church can have measurable success without ever directly challenging the powers of darkness" (p. 12). That's a powerful statement. And it's true. We can enjoy a measure of blessing without ever encroaching upon the enemy's territory.

If you are willing to be satisfied with just an acre of land, the enemy will gladly relent that acre to you. Why? He will do that because you are contained, and you won't encroach on his territory. You're not interested in expanding and taking new territory. You're not going to put a demand on him to return, with interest, the things he stole from you through injustices or sins. He'll be *glad* to give you an acre for the trade out of keeping you from the greater things that have been assigned to your life and generation. The question is: Do you want to continue in a maintenance mentality, or would you rather stand up, push back against the darkness and gain new territory, taking what is rightfully yours spiritually?

Having success spiritually means establishing the Kingdom

here on earth. Establishing the Kingdom — what does that mean? It means establishing Christ, or, in other words, getting grounded personally in your relationship with Christ—and grounding your principles and key areas of your life in Christ as well. It means raising a standard where there has been moral decay, personally or in a place or family. It means baptizing in grace where sin abounds.

To have a real impact in our generation (our personal lives, our families, cities, nations), we have to understand the powers of darkness are there and must be confronted. If you have been completely frustrated, feeling like every time you get going the rug gets pulled out from under your feet, I can assure you that your wrestling is not against that person or system with which you are having problems. There is a battle going on, and the only way you will win it is by bearing spiritual arms and by taking authority and dominion over what is happening in the spirit realm, thereby arresting what is happening or manifesting itself in the public place. This is the principle of binding and loosing we see mentioned in Matthew 18:18.

I want to give you 10 very simple strategies for successfully engaging in spiritual warfare. I know there are scores of books available that address this theme even more profoundly than I will attempt here. My intent is to give you, within the scheme of this book, some starting points in the areas of spiritual warfare. (I have purposely omitted the subject of fasting from this list because I want to cover it in more detail later—but it plays a vital role in spiritual warfare and our spiritual development.)

What are some practical steps that you can take to begin to confront strongholds in your life that are impeding your spiritual growth or advancement?

1. Time in the secret place

The secret place is essentially personal time spent with the Lord in prayer, in worship and in meditation of Scripture. It's time for just you and God. Everyone has his or her own way of entering into the presence of the Lord. I start with worship. I usually put worship music on in the background. I'm selective about the music I play during my time with the Lord. I want it to be full of the Word and full of the Spirit. I love music that's pregnant with the prophetic—in other words, it speaks to my spirit in a deep way or speaks of things to come.

Worship usually gives way to more specific praying.

I am a pacer. I pace when I pray. Others prefer to sit with their Bible open on their lap. I walk with my Bible in my hands—I might feel led to pause or to turn off the music if I sense the Holy Spirit wants to speak something into my heart. I often feel directed to specific Scriptures during my time in worship and prayer. When that happens, I generally pray those Scripture back to the Lord—or declare it against the enemy.

The formula isn't important (whether you sit, kneel, pace or lie on your face praying)—what's important is the intimacy, the relationship and the communication with the Lord. The secret place isn't really a place at all; rather, it is time where we allow the Holy Spirit to speak to us. This is very important because Romans 8:27 says, "And he who searches our hearts knows the mind of the Spirit, because the Spirit intercedes for the saints in accordance with God's will." When we have time with the Lord, we benefit from it because the Holy Spirit is praying *through* us and *for* us according to the will of God. And the will of God, in one way or another, will be communicated to our heart and mind through the Word, through prayer or through the Spirit speaking directly into our hearts as we spend time with Him.

If the formula you've used to get into the presence of the Lord hasn't been effective—change it! Try putting on music in the background or try a different kind of music. If you want different results than what you've gotten so far, you have to change what you've been doing up until now.

Another thing to remember is this: Prayer isn't a once a day thing! I can't count the times I've heard someone say, "I don't even have an hour to myself every day. How am I supposed to get alone for an hour to be with the Lord?"

Friend, prayer is conversation with God. There have been many times where my ministry schedule has been so tight I found myself without any alone time with the Lord. One of those times was when I was on an airplane. I thought, *I'm finally going to have about 10 hours of down time! Yay for no cell phones on flights!* But then I had the quandary of not being able to pray out loud. I thought, *This person next to me is going to think I'm nuts if I sit here talking to God!* So, I got up and went to the restroom. They'd already turned the lights out on the plane so that people could sleep, so I thought, *This is perfect—no one will be getting up to go to the restroom—I'll have my prayer time in the airplane restroom!* So, that's what I did. I had an awesome time in prayer there in that tiny restroom. I couldn't pace like I normally do, but hey—at least I had some alone time! I think I turned three shades of red when I finally exited the restroom and saw people lined up halfway to the back of the plane waiting to get in. They did not have happy expressions on their faces!

The point is this: Prayer happens wherever and whenever you begin to speak to the Lord. Create the opportunities. Tune your ear in to Him. Worship when you have a window of opportunity. Enrich your spirit and plug into the presence of the Lord! Why? Because when you pray, you are being effective against the enemy! When you pray, you are strengthening the resolve of your own spirit against your flesh! When you pray, you are pushing back darkness and establishing boundaries to the enemy by administrating your God-given authority! In essence, when we pray, we are cooperating with the Spirit of God, the will of God and the hosts of heaven who battle on our behalf! When we begin cooperating in the natural, the things of the Spirit begin to manifest on earth!

2. Pray for revelation (ask God to reveal things to you)!

Jeremiah 33:3 says that we can ask Him, and He will answer us and show us things that we do not know.

I remember when it finally occurred to me I could ask God to reveal things to me. I was serving under my mentor's ministry, and I remember seeing firsthand the gifts of the Spirit in action through him. He moved powerfully in the prophetic. I remember him talking to those of us whom he was mentoring and him encouraging us to ask God to speak to us in our dreams. I had such a hunger for the authentic—I had been so disillusioned with the spiritually platonic, that I immediately took hold of that challenge and began to ask the Lord to speak to me in dreams and through the gifts of the Spirit. And He did. It was quite amazing. He was gracious to a young novice, and I suppose He rewarded my childlike faith. I remember soon after that the Lord gave me a dream about a situation that was happening in the church. It was something hidden, and nobody in the natural knew what was driving a certain situation we were seeing within the congregation. God revealed it to me in a dream. *It wasn't given to me so that I could go public with the information. God spoke to me through a dream in order to equip me with the wisdom I would need to deal with a very delicate situation.* I was not blindsided by the situation when it was finally time to confront it, but was prepared and even felt the Lord had given me a strategy to handle it.

I could cite other times where the Lord has spoken to my heart and given me wisdom and insight into complex situations through the gifts of the Spirit or through a dream. I have already told how the Lord revealed things to me as I was fasting in 1998. God has frequently directed me or even given me prophetic insight into things, which were about to unfold in my life or ministry, while I was fasting.

Are these things really for today? Well, if we say we live under the new covenant (the New Testament—the order that Jesus set into place spiritually through His redemptive intervention in time and humanity), why would we only partake of it in part? Salvation through Jesus was the great door opener for us to come close to God and have a personal relationship with Him. In John 14:16 and 18, Jesus also told us He would send a Helper, a Counselor, and a Comforter (the Holy Spirit), so we would not be left orphans (or without guidance, care and provision). I hunger to see all of the Word fulfilled and functioning in my life. Including the promises of God regarding the miraculous and the gifts of the Spirit as outlined in I Corinthians 12. The gifts of the Spirit or revelation by the Holy Spirit are not reserved for an exclusive few—the Holy Spirit desires to be in relationship and communion with each one of us.

In Daniel 2:27 and 28a, Daniel told King Nebuchadnezzar, "No wise man, enchanter, magician or diviner can explain to the king the mystery he has asked about, *but there is a God in heaven who reveals mysteries*". God still reveals mysteries when we look to Him for answers! If we believe God has not changed, then we must believe in the full Word of God, and that God, who historically always spoke and revealed things to His people, will still act in the same way today—if His people will call on Him and seek Him.

You may be facing a situation in your business or in your family, and you have no idea what action to take. You may be at a crossroad in your life where you are looking behind you at the things that have always determined your path or set your boundaries, and you are looking out ahead of you into your future, and you are realizing how badly you desire change, but you don't even know where to start. Friend, God will guide you, give you strategies, and give you answers. Don't take action in the natural until you take action in prayer!

I Corinthians 2:10 emphasizes that God is able, through the Holy Spirit, to reveal things to us: "*these are the things God has revealed to us by his Spirit.* The Spirit searches all things, even the deep things of God."

There are deep things God knows about you and great things He has planned for you. When you begin to pray and ask Him to give you understanding, revelation and guidance, the Holy Spirit will answer that prayer. I'm not encouraging you to be mystical, but I *am* saying that in times of spiritual impasse, in times where change is needed, in times where it's obvious a spiritual battle is raging, it's imperative for us to have the mind of God on the matter. The freedom we have to ask this of the Lord is part of our benefits as children of God.

Tap into the Spirit — don't wait on things to magically fall into place. Destiny happens by choice, not chance. Be proactive and ask for revelation and wisdom—even in your process of restoration and healing!

3. Get others engaged with you

You should have some go-to people in your life — people you can depend on and look to for help in prayer. I'm talking about covenant-type relationships. People who are committed to you—to seeing you move forward, healed and restored. People who believe in the call of God on your life and who believe in your vision and dreams.

These should be trustworthy, emotionally mature, spiritually wise and discerning people. They will be few, not many! I'm not talking about a prayer chain! And, by discerning, I'm not referring to people who are suspicious. There's a world of difference between discernment and suspicion. One is a gift of the spirit (discerning of spirits), and one is just, well — of the flesh! One can bring life. The other can damage, wound and destroy.

Look for people who are farther along than you are in your walk with the Lord, or, people who are at least at the same level you are. Remember—you want people who understand prayer, who know how to hear from the Lord, who know the Word of God. These will be people you can call upon when you are in a time of decision, when you are stuck, when you are desperate for answers or change. *Enlist them in the battle with you!* There is power in numbers, especially when it comes to prayer. I will often send out an e-mail to a select group of people when I sense we are under attack as a ministry, or when I sense there is a change coming. I also send it out when I'm just plain exhausted and can't fight by myself. I can tell you firsthand accounts of times when, after enlisting others to pray for me and for my situation, there was a night-and-day difference or a major turnaround in my situation. I've also asked them to pray for me when I've needed an answer from the Lord on something. And, many times, I've received direction through some of those trusted intercessors.

I remember when I injured my back while living in Thailand. I herniated a disk and had another one bulging about to rupture. I have always been athletic and loved being active, so this injury was devastating to me. By the end of one week, I couldn't walk. I was hospitalized and had a group of Thai Buddhist surgeons coming into my hospital room every day for a week telling me I "would not be able to get up and walk out of this hospital without surgery." I almost believed them, as I lay there unable to even turn to one side or the other. There were other things happening at that same time in my ministry. We were experiencing intense spiritual attacks and conflicts. I was overwhelmed.

I refused to let them operate. A week later, I managed to get up and limp out of the hospital, still in severe pain. After a month, I was still basically homebound. I could not sit for over five minutes at a time without extreme pain. I felt depressed, but it went beyond depression. There was an oppression that was almost palpable. I lived in a building owned by Hindus, with Hindu gods and idols everywhere in the passageways, and a Buddhist spirit altar at the entrance of the building. From a nearby Muslim mosque, I could hear the Imam reciting his prayers over a loud speaker several times a day—quite a heavy-duty environment. I felt debilitated, not just physically, but spiritually as well. I longed to go to the airport and board the next plane to the United States, but I was determined to stick it out!

I got on the phone and called the States and started asking for intercessors to being covering me. I e-mailed my go-to people. Why I hadn't done it sooner, I have no idea! There was an *immediate* turnaround in my situation. I began to improve physically. I began to feel that horrible oppression lift. When I involved other people in my push against darkness, it was as if people were literally holding my arms up and carrying me. They fought for me when I was too weak to fight for myself. It gave me a respite to breathe, gather my strength and see the situation through. Had I not involved others, there would have been a totally different outcome.

That's just one small example of how involving key prayer people in my battle brought a breakthrough. Our Aguas de Sanidad (the name of my ministry, which means Healing Waters) team has many times reaped the benefit of getting others engaged with us in prayer at key moments. While in Rome, Italy, we seemed to be facing difficulty and frustration even in the simplest things in our ministry trip. I had a very vivid dream one night where the Lord was showing me that what we were struggling against was a spiritual resistance— spiritual warfare, not simply natural resistance from people or situations. That same morning Graciela got up saying she also sensed the need to intercede and come against principalities and powers, even those of the region. We got on Skype and called trusted friends and got them engaged in prayer with us. One of them, as he prayed for us over Skype, gave us a word of wisdom that really helped us. From that moment, things began to turn around in the trip.

I often ask those who are praying for our ministry team or me to e-mail me if they sense anything in prayer. This principle of engaging others in spiritual warfare prayer has also been key in my own personal journey. I am so thankful for key people whom I have been able to fully trust in personal matters of prayer.

Remember: Your go-to people will be few, not many. They should be spiritually mature people who know how to touch God in prayer and how to hear from the Lord.

4. Learn the art of listening

One of the most important and critical things every believer needs is to learn how to hear and recognize the voice of the Lord. If you want an intimate daily walk with the Lord, recognizing His voice is imperative. If you want to successfully confront and defeat strongholds in your life, learning how to hear from the Lord is the key.

When I was a little girl, maybe 9 years old, my girl's club director at church asked me if I would share something for our devotions the next week. It was something that would mark my life. I remember going home and asking my mom how to know for sure what I was to talk about? She told me the Lord would speak to my heart. "Well, how do I know it's Him?" I asked her.

She said, "You just go in to your bedroom tonight, and while you are lying on your bed, ask Jesus to show you something from the Bible—He'll bring something to your mind that you haven't necessarily thought of before. You'll know it's Him. Just ask Him. He'll speak to you."

So, as I crawled into bed that night, I lay there with

my arms folded behind my head, staring at the ceiling and prayed. It was simple, actually. I did just what my mom told me to do. And as I lay there thinking, asking Jesus to show me something from the Word, to speak to my heart, I began to think about Peter walking on the water. I pictured him on the water. I pictured Jesus in front of him. Then it's like I just saw the whole thing in another perspective. The Lord showed me that the water represented everything in life, including sin, which can intimidate us and make us take our eyes off Jesus. When we take our eyes off Jesus, we sink. But in the same way Jesus lifted Peter up out of the waves of the churning sea when he cried out to Him, He will rescue us from the world and from sin when we cry out to Him. Hey, it wasn't a three-point sermon, but it was revelation to this 9-year-old little girl! And I just knew that the Lord had dropped that into my mind. As simple as this illustration might seem to you, it was something that changed my own life as a little girl. I suddenly knew God would speak to me if I asked, and if I listened.

Knowing how to recognize the voice of the Lord and familiarizing yourself with how He speaks to you is something that will absolutely revolutionize your walk with God. The key is *listening*. It's an art. It's something that is refined through process and time.

The priest, Eli, taught his young novice, Samuel, how to recognize the voice of the Lord. Samuel already had the capacity to hear—he *heard* someone call him, but he didn't recognize who it was, nor would he have understood how to linger and *listen* to what God had to say had Eli not instructed him.

In I Samuel 3:7 we see that "Samuel did not yet know the LORD: The word of the LORD had not yet been revealed to him." The word, *know,* in that verse means *to recognize or be acquainted with.* The phrase, *the word of the Lord* literally means the voice of God—His speaking and utterance. Notice when Samuel recognized God's voice, then God could fully speak to Him. We have to recognize His voice before He can speak anything to us. If we do not recognize His voice, we shrug off His inner promptings and instantly shut our ears down. The Bible tells us that God continued to speak to Samuel in Shiloh. Shiloh was the place where Samuel knew He would hear from God. He familiarized himself with that place, as well as with the voice of the Lord.

Once you begin to develop your prayer life, you'll also begin to recognize how the Holy Spirit speaks to you. Prayer will no longer be you doing all the talking, but you'll also begin to take time to be silent in order to listen to what the Lord might want to say to you. Not everything that enters into our mind is from God—even in times of prayer. But over time, as you develop the disciplines of prayer and time in the Word, it becomes easier to distinguish between your own thoughts and the voice of the Holy Spirit. Like Samuel with Shiloh, you will cherish your secret place with the Lord, and you will know how to hear from Him there.

5. Take dominion: Declare and establish by your mouth!

There were so many times in the past when I questioned the necessity of declaring something out loud in prayer. I wondered if it was really necessary to declare, "I bind" or "I take dominion." As I was thinking about this, I thought about Ezekiel 37.

Ezekiel 37 is an amazing account of the Spirit of the Lord

appearing to Ezekiel and taking him and setting him down in a valley full of dry bones. The only thing I can relate that to is the multiple times I went into Cambodia and saw thousands of skulls and bones stacked in memorial to the millions who died during the cruel reign of the Cambodian dictator, Pol Pot. I can only imagine how the prophet Ezekiel must have felt being led back and forth *among* the bones in that valley (Ezek. 37:1, 2).

Bones represent death. They also represent a life lived. Bones leave a sense of loss or of potential cut short. They can speak to what could've been, and even what should have been.

Once the Spirit of the Lord had sufficiently demonstrated to the prophet the dryness and lifelessness of the bones, he then asked him a question: Can these bones live? Is there hope for these dried up representations of lives lost? Ezekiel said, "Lord, only you know the answer to that!" (Ezek. 37:3)

So the Spirit of the Lord said to him,

> *Prophecy to these bones and say to them, 'Dry bones, hear the word of the Lord!* This is what the Sovereign LORD says to these bones: I will make breath enter you, and you will come to life. I will attach tendons to you and make flesh come upon you and cover you with skin; I will put breath in you, and you will come to life. Then you will know that I am the LORD'
>
> –EZEKIEL 37:4-6

So, Ezekiel said, "I prophesied as I was commanded. *And as I was prophesying*, there was a noise, a rattling sound, and the bones came together, bone to bone." (Ezek. 37:7)

Like Ezekiel out amongst those bones, our reality can be overwhelming. When we enter into our prayer time, and we're seeing dry bones all around us, it's hard to have faith that life can come back into something that has seemingly died. That's why it's important to *prophecy and declare* the word of the Lord! Notice the Spirit of the Lord told Ezekiel to say, "Dry bones, *hear* the word of the Lord!" The enemy needs to *hear* us declaring the Word of the Lord out loud! The Word is the sword of the Spirit (Eph. 6:17), so when we speak and declare it—we're swinging our sword! When we begin to speak things in prayer, we are essentially taking authority over the enemy, which establishes *limits* on his power!

Not only is declaring the Word out loud effective against the enemy, it also is effective against doubt, intimidation and personal fear! I speak Scriptures out loud to combat my own doubts and fears! I speak them to remind myself and to remind the enemy of who has the final word in the situation!

When Ezekiel prophesied (when He *declared*) what he heard the Spirit of the Lord say, he took dominion over impossibilities and established the will of the Lord for those dried up bones. He brought life!

God has given *you* the authority to establish His will through declaring (administrating) the Word of the Lord over your situation, your family, your ministry and your future.

In my enthusiasm to encourage you to declare the Word out loud in prayer, let me also encourage you to not go to extremes on this point! I have friends who have taken this principle to such extremes that it's become bondage to them and to those around them. As I've said many times already, don't allow yourself to become mystical. I know people who will react histrionically, for example, if someone says something like, "Well, you know, it's the hottest day of the year, which means the A/C will probably go out!"

Immediately, they will rebuke the person, saying, "Don't speak that over your life or your air conditioner!" It's true, we need to guard what we say and guard against negativity. But, not *everything* that I speak is going to come to come to pass! Yet, when I speak *the Word of the Lord*, the Bible tells us that His Word will not return void to Him, *but will accomplish everything for which He sent it out to do.*

He's the God who gives life to the dead and calls those things that are not as though they were (Rom. 4:17)! We are His voice here in the earthly realm—so open your mouth to declare, prophecy and call those things that are not as though they were! Establish it by declaration in prayer!

6. Learn the importance of retreat

Having grown up the only girl with two older brothers, it was almost an obligation to participate in my brothers' pretend world of cowboys and Indians (a major part of the history of my own country of the United States). We learned through TV movies how to properly fight in pretend scenarios of being surrounded by Indians, or, if playing the role of Indians, by cowboys. At some time during the intensity of whatever make-believe battle we were desperately trying to win, somebody would invariably yell out, "*Retreat! Retreat!*" Everybody on our side would then quickly run away and return to camp so we could regroup and rethink our battle strategy.

Those were childhood games and scenarios. But, unknowingly, we'd picked up on a really important real life battle strategy: Learning when to retreat.

Before George Washington served as first President of the United States of America, he was General Washington. He has gone down in history as one of the most brilliant war strategists ever known. In the American Revolution when America was trying to gain its independence from Great Britain, Washington took command of a fledgling army of peasants, farmers, merchants and fishermen. They numbered no more than 18,000 men. They were confronted in New York in the Battle of Long Island (August, 1776) by 300-400 British ships and more than 30,000 veteran British soldiers. They were completely outgunned and outnumbered. The accepted rule of engagement of that day was face-to-face line combat. But, being the brilliant strategist that he was, Washington refused to play by the enemy's rules. Instead of continuing in a losing battle, he did what would've, at that time, seemed like the unthinkable: He retreated — secretly. He called for every kind of boat and floating vessel possible and gathered them under cover of darkness and dense fog, and silently began to remove his men and supplies from the battlefront. This retreat would be key to Washington eventually leading America to a victory against the British, gaining America her independence as a nation. Washington recognized it was unwise to continue exhausting precious supplies in a setting that would not ultimately give way to productive victory. So, he retreated. He took his guns, his supplies and his team, and he left the battleground. He didn't check out of the war. He just began to choose his fights more wisely. That retreat allowed him and his troops the time they needed to regain their footing, receive additional supplies and be joined by additional troops. They were able to move to an area where they could fight their kind of fight on their own terrain and their own terms. And the retreat set them up for victory.[1]

---

1   "George Washington: Commander In Chief" http://www.ushistory.org/valleyforge/washington/george2.html

In a letter he wrote, Washington penned six battle strategies by which he lived as a wartime leader. I want to share two of those strategies with you as we talk about the importance of retreat in times of battle:

> Never attack a position in front, which you can gain by turning. Never do what the enemy wishes you to do.

When you are blindsided by the enemy by an unexpected attack, the natural tendency is to immediately jump up and engage the enemy by reacting. This is a favorite battle strategy of Satan known as distraction! In the book of Nehemiah, we see this strategy in action very clearly! When Nehemiah was finally engaged in rebuilding the destroyed wall of Jerusalem, when he finally had the people inspired and a great team assembled, two troublemakers, named Sanballat and Tobias, sent letters to him urging (intimidating) him to leave the work and meet with them. They escalated the threats and bullying when Nehemiah refused to leave the work. Instead of going down to engage the enemy on the *enemy's* terms, Nehemiah refused to even step onto the battlefield. Nehemiah refused to do what the enemy wished him to do! He changed his strategy and had the workers carry a sword in one hand and a weapon in the other (never attack a position in front, which you can gain by turning).

Sometimes the enemy wants to exhaust our strength and resources by sending us into a panic and evoking an immediate reaction, trying to obligate us to engage in a fight with him. But, like Washington, we need godly wisdom to know when it would be wiser to preserve our strength for a timely push at another time or in another place. The Holy Spirit will give you wisdom to know when it's time to fight or when you are better served by retreating and taking shelter in Him.

"The name of the Lord is a strong tower; the righteous run to it and are safe" (Prov. 18:10).

7. Know your enemy!

There are a lot of Christians who fall into the trap of wanting to study and know all about the devil. That does not describe how I feel. Anything I need to know about devil, I believe I will find in the Bible. I want to know about Jesus. I want to know the Word of God.

Yet, having said that, I do believe it's necessary to know what you are dealing with in times of spiritual warfare! There are times when we absolutely need to know what the enemy is up to and what we are dealing with!

I won't take a lot of time under this point because I have covered a lot of what I would like to share here in other chapters. Remember the story that I related about the woman (Satanist) who was cursing me as I preached at a women's conference in the States? That was one of those times when it was necessary for me to know what was happening and how to come against it! My friend Graciela and I specifically prayed that God would expose the enemy—and He did! It didn't take a rocket scientist to figure out that I was under a spiritual attack, but I needed to know what the spiritual attack was and how to pray against it! The lady came up to me after the next morning's service and confessed everything to me. After that, we were able to better guard ourselves from a continued attack over the course of the next weekend's conference as well.

II Corinthians 2:11 talks about not being ignorant of Satan's schemes. Satan is a schemer. There are times when it's important to remember his modus operandi. When you are having difficulty seeing a breakthrough in a certain city or region, it's important to get a handle on the enemy and his schemes! When you can't get a handle on what is driving a certain situation, begin to ask the Lord to expose the enemy, his work or the root of the cause of the resistance against the work of God. God will give you wisdom, and will expose the enemy so you can fight smarter and more effectively!

8. Forgive and provide restoration whenever possible

To many this point might seem like an error in my list! I mean we *are* talking about 10 strategies for successfully engaging in spiritual warfare, right? What does forgiveness and restoration have to do with spiritual warfare?

They have everything to do with the subject, actually. On a personal and a corporate level, forgiving and providing restoration are such effective ways of defeating one of Satan's greatest weapons against the church and against us personally as believers — division.

Let me borrow another one of Washington's six battle strategies mentioned in point six. One of his six strategies for battle was: Nothing is so important in war as an undivided command. *Undivided.* He understood how critical it was to be undivided when going up against the enemy.

Jesus said in Matthew 12:25, "Every kingdom *divided against* itself is brought to desolation, and every city or *house divided* against itself *will not stand.*" There's nothing as debilitating within the Body of Christ as division. Remember, we are dealing with two realms: The heavenly places and the earth or natural realm. One directly affects the other! You can't have division in one without it impacting the other.

A couple of years ago our team was organizing a huge conference in a province here in Argentina. All of our events are interdenominational, and we work with a plethora of organizations, both secular and Christian. So, it's sometimes a real challenge for the leaders who get involved in the promotion and organization of the event to work together cohesively.

In this particular event, we knew early on that we were going to face a lot of spiritual warfare. The venue we were going to use, from its inauguration, had been dedicated not just to the public, but also to cults in the region. Multiple cult ceremonies and sacrifices had been performed on the grounds. Even when I took a friend with me to talk to the office manager about the costs of renting the venue, we had to stop and minister to the person because they started manifesting demons when we came into their office. That was our first clue that we were intruding on the enemy's turf.

We were entering into the final week before the conference. I got a phone call from some of the point people who were handling the details in the province. They called to tell me that half of them were quitting and would not allow people from their churches to participate in the conference. There were hurt feelings, anger, misunderstanding, and the whole thing appeared to be imploding. Mind you, I'm not talking about the unbelievers involved in the organization of the event. I'm talking about the different church leaders and helpers who had come together to help us. To top things off, I had a team arriving the next day from the States to participate and help at the event. I had to make the tough decision to make the long trip up to the province to meet with all the parties involved. That meant that I wouldn't even be able to be at the airport to receive the team coming in from my home state. I was torn about it, but I knew what I needed to do. I knew that this was not a fight of flesh and blood, but it was a spiritual attack. Not one of the people involved in the conflicts were bad. I love and respect them all to this day. But the enemy had woven division into the group and was about to destroy our efforts before we even had a chance to minister! The assistant leader of Aguas and I headed up to meet with the group. The discussion between the different parties was heated! I didn't have any wise profound answers. Just one thing occurred to me. As I was listening to one of the leaders expressing her feelings, God helped me to understand the hurt behind the anger. I felt the Lord put something in my heart to do, but wow, I was so hesitant to do it! I didn't know what reaction I might get. But I did it anyway. I got up and walked to the other side of the conference table where she was seated, and I leaned down and told her how sorry I was that everything had unfolded as it had, and that we would have never had it happen like that. I told her how much we cared and how much her efforts were valued. And then —I threw the big hug on her! She hugged back.

Then something extraordinary happened. Her whole tone and attitude softened. She reached out to those who had offended her. And they essentially hugged back. It was an amazing moment. It was something very loving in the natural, but we were throwing deadly blows to the head of the enemy in the spirit! We were unbarring the gates of his citadel through forgiveness and restoration. Proverbs 18:19 says, "An offended brother is more unyielding than a fortified city, and disputes are like the barred gates of a citadel." There is strength in numbers and in unity, especially in the Body of Christ. Nothing will abort a God-given vision faster than division.

Oh, the rest of that story goes like this: The day of the event when the worship team began the first song, literally, demons began to cry out as people controlled by them ran forward asking to be set free! We saw more deliverance in that event than all of our other events combined! The attendance was double the capacity of the venue, and we ministered for 16 hours that day and well into the night! The provincial pastoral committee contacted us after the event to tell us that never in the history of that province had an event left such an impact within the Body of Christ. They excitedly told us how people from different churches and ministries who would hardly speak before the event were now gathering on a weekly basis to eat together, visit and pray! Many of those people are the ones who had sat around the table that day when tensions were high and offenses rampant. Forgiveness and restoration had broken the chains of the enemy and empowered the Body of Christ to be effective in bringing a breakthrough to their region!

Friend, sometimes it's easier to have a burden and love for the person on the street, the prostitute on the corner, the needy poverty stricken children in the missionary's video than it is to forgive someone who has offended us—especially a fellow believer. It may *feel* easier to leave a situation unresolved and let the relationship deteriorate, but the end results are devastating. Restoration and forgiveness bring breakthrough and advancement. Do you want to grow and mature spiritually? Restore. Forgive. You will unbar the gates of the enemy's citadel and usher in such peace and growth in your life. It will overflow into blessing and authority in your ministry and personal journey! Forgiveness is a hammer that crushes the control of the enemy. I'm praying as I close out this point, that the Holy Spirit will use this to bring restoration to broken friendships and relationships in your life, church, family or city. Forgiveness and restoration is worth the work.

9. Pray in the Spirit

I believe that it is as equally important to pray in the Spirit as it is to pray with understanding. Paul concluded that he would do both (I Cor. 14).

We can declare things we understand by praying Scripture out loud. We're praying with understanding, as Paul put it. But there's something powerful about praying in the Spirit. Paul says in I Corinthians 14:2, 4, *"For he who speaks in a tongue does not speak to men but to God, for no one understands him; however, in the spirit he speaks mysteries. He who speaks in a tongue edifies himself,* but he who prophesies edifies the church."

Ephesians 6 outlines the armor of God, and how we should bear arms against the enemy. Included in that passage is verse 18 that says, that we should be "praying always with all prayer and supplication *in the Spirit"*

Romans 8:26 and 27 says, "In the same way, *the Spirit helps us* in our weakness. *We do not know what we ought to pray for, but the Spirit himself intercedes for us* through wordless groans. And he who searches our hearts knows the mind of the Spirit, *because the Spirit intercedes for God's people in accordance with the will of God.*

Jude 20 and 21 says, "But you, beloved, building yourselves up on your most holy faith, *praying in the Holy Spirit,* keep yourselves in the love of God, looking for the mercy of our Lord Jesus Christ unto eternal life."

When you are out of words—pray in the Spirit! When you need strength—pray in the Spirit! When you are pushing against darkness and needing a breakthrough, but you don't have any more answers or words—pray in the Spirit! It's a spiritual weapon of war and should be a part of your time with the Lord throughout the day. You will reap personal benefits, but also are allowing the Holy Spirit to declare things according to the will of God through your own mouth!

10. Rest in the goodness of God

We put a lot of emphasis on *doing* in this generation. But the thing that sets you up for overcoming isn't anything that you have already done or anything that you will do in the future. It's all about being — *being* a child of God. It's about what *God did* for you. He rescued you by something *He did.* He doesn't love you because you are doing the right things. He loves you because you are his child. You didn't earn His love. He loved you just because you're you and He wanted closeness with you. You have his blessing.

So even in the scheme of spiritual warfare and all that we've discussed in the previous nine strategies, this strategy is my favorite, and, in my opinion, probably the most effective. What is it? It's simply this: Rest in the goodness of God. Depend on His goodness and the track record of His faithfulness. Depend on His strength. Depend on His already clenched victory over the enemy. Relax in Him. Stop struggling and hide yourself in Him. Let Him do it for you.

I think the Word expresses it best. I encourage you to read over these Scriptures and then stop. Lean your head back, close your eyes, take a deep breath and rest in the Lord's goodness. Really — take some time right now to meditate on these verses and then speak them over yourself. Let yourself rest and depend on His greatness to see you through this time in your life. He will fight for you. He's just good like that.

Find rest, O my soul, in God alone; my hope comes from him (Psa. 62:5).

I wait for the LORD, my soul waits, and in his word I put my hope (Psa. 130:5).

Be still, and know that I am God; I will be exalted among the nations, I will be exalted in the earth (Psa. 46:10).

Come to me, all you who are weary and burdened, and I will give you rest (Matt. 11:28).

But those who hope in the LORD will renew their strength. They will soar on wings like eagles; they will run and not grow weary, they will walk and not be faint (Isa. 40:31).

LORD, you establish peace for us; all that we have accomplished you have done for us (Isa. 26:12).

This is one of my personal favorites: Psalm 23.

The LORD is my shepherd, I shall not be in want.
He makes me lie down in green pastures, He leads me beside quiet waters,
He restores my soul. He guides me in paths of righteousness for His name's sake.
Even though I walk through the valley of the shadow of death,

I will fear no evil, for You are with me; Your rod and Your staff, they comfort me.

You prepare a table before me in the presence of my enemies. You anoint my head with oil; my cup overflows.

Surely goodness and love will follow me all the days of my life, and I will dwell in the house of the LORD forever.

CHAPTER 5

THE POWER OF FASTING

Fasting is an indispensable tool and a powerful weapon in spiritual warfare.

My life would be so different if I had not been taught about fasting. It has played a key role in the most pivotal points of my life. I'm thankful for Pastor Randy Clark, who, back in 1991, took a Sunday morning service and taught on fasting. He was my pastor at that time. That Sunday morning message changed my walk with God. I had never heard anyone teach about fasting, and was totally unaware that it could be such a transforming discipline in the life of every believer.

Pastor Clark taught from a key passage of Scripture that Sunday: Isaiah 58. In the beginning of this chapter God is bringing correction to His people. In verses 3 through 5, He says,

They ask me for decisions and seem eager for God to come near them. 'Why have we fasted,' they say, 'and you have not seen it? Why have we humbled ourselves and you have not noticed?' Yet on the day of your fasting, you do as you please and exploit all your workers. Your fasting ends in quarreling and strife… You cannot fast as you do today and expect your voice to be heard on high. Is this the kind of fast I have chosen, only a day for a man to humble himself? Is it only for bowing one's head like a reed and for lying on sackcloth and ashes? Is that what you call a fast, a day acceptable to the Lord?"

Fasting is more than just not eating. As the preceding verses demonstrate, God was not pleased with fasting as a religious ritual, something being used to force the hand of God. It had turned into presumption on the part of the people towards God. They were saying, "If I don't eat, You have to do this or that for me."

The first thing to understand about fasting is that it does not always yield a quick fix or immediate response from the Lord every time we do it. Fasting, many times, has to do with an inner work that needs to happen within us. There have been many times when I fasted seeking a change in my situation only to see my circumstance stay the same. Instead, God did something in *me* that caused me to be able to rise above what I was faced with. I was able to move on in spite of a negative situation or opposition.

Fasting should *activate* something in our lives. It will generate something on the inside of a person—freedom from oppression, breaking of yokes, loosing of chains, your night turning into light, healing, closeness with the Lord, satisfaction, strength, restoration, raising up something from the ruins, joy in your relationship with God, and peace in your relationships with others (verses 6-14). And then it will inspire action *towards* others—loosing the chains of injustice, setting the oppressed free, sharing food with the hungry and providing the poor with shelter, clothing the naked, and responding to your family's needs.

Two Kinds of Fasts

I have found that there are two major kinds of fasting. The first kind is fasting as a discipline of one's spiritual life. We abstain from food for a spiritual purpose. We refrain from eating in order to discipline our flesh—our carnality. So much of what we do is a direct result of what we have in our mind and emotions. Many times our life is full of consequences of being guided by emotions and an undisciplined mind. Fasting is a way to strengthen our spirit and take dominion over our mind, emotions and even our body. Fasting should be viewed as a natural partner of prayer and the Word. The three go hand in hand. Fasting, as a regular discipline helps us maintain our spiritual growth and sensitivity to the Holy Spirit. There is also a greater spiritual authority that comes through a lifestyle of fasting. When I say lifestyle, I'm referring to a personal decision to fast on a regular basis, whether it's once a week, once a month or whatever.

The second kind of fasting is a designated fast. This is a fast done for a specific purpose or need. I believe it can be self-declared, or it can be something the Holy Spirit prompts you to do. Although fasting is always a challenge, during designated fasts I have found that there is an unusual grace to be able to complete it.

I grew up watching western movies that almost always depicted stories of the relationship between North American cowboys and Indians. There's one scene that I can picture in my mind to this day. It's a scene where an Indian scout is riding with a group of cowboy lawmen. The whole group has stopped, and the Indian dismounts his horse. He gets on his hands and knees, bends over and puts his ear down to the ground. The cowboys are looking at each other like, *What's he doing?* It's a popular scene found in many western movies. It's also quite accurate historically. You see, the Indian understood how to discern and hear things that no one else could hear. He could *feel* what was coming. He could *hear* what was coming. He could even *discern*, many times, *what* was coming even before human eyes had sight of it!

Fasting is just like that! Fasting is putting your ear down to the ground. Fasting helps us to hear, sense and discern things that are, many times, unseen. Fasting is a prophetic tool, as well. In other words, through fasting, many times, the Lord will help us discern what is to come.

When I begin a designated fast, I always take three index cards (ok, these days I use my computer, but for the sake of better explanation, I'll use the index cards as an example!), and I title them like this:

Objective of My Fast
Directive Scriptures
Directive Thoughts

I have found that it's really important to write things down during a fast. I start out with my first card: Objective of My Fast. Why am I fasting? What do I hope for or what is it that I need or want to see accomplished? This helps keep me focused in prayer during my fast.

The second card is titled Directive Scriptures. On this, I write down significant Scriptures that I feel directed to read while praying during my fast. Remember, fasting is not just abstaining from food. It's purposefully seeking God in prayer and the Word during times when you would normally be eating, and maintaining that same level of spiritual attention even outside of mealtimes during the duration of your fast.

Finally, there is my third card, on which I write thoughts or ideas I feel the Holy Spirit is speaking to me as I fast and pray. There's a very good possibility that at some time in our lives we have mislabeled the voice of God as being our own thoughts. By dismissing something we sense in our hearts, we can actually miss hearing the voice of God. That's why it's a good idea to write down your thoughts as you pray during your fast.

At the end of a fast, I can usually see a story unfolding within the content of my three index cards. There's usually a clear parallel between my second and third card. In other words, the things I felt the Lord speaking into my mind during my fast will line up with the Scriptures He directed me to. If you don't write it down, you'll forget it and might lose vital details the Lord was weaving together over the course of your fast.

So, what happens when we fast?

Fasting is effective in three ways: It is a weapon of spiritual warfare; it is a way by which we petition God; and it is a tool that helps keep us sensitized to the Lord.

Fasting: A Weapon of Spiritual Warfare

Fasting breaks through obstructions in the spirit. When you fast, you are doing battle.

In Daniel 10, we read about a vision that God gave Daniel. The vision was so complex and so extreme that it left Daniel absolutely disturbed. He saw the vision, he knew it was something very serious, but he didn't have understanding of what he saw. He felt an urgency to seek understanding. So he began to fast. He fasted meats and sweets for 21 days (there are many who have extended and detailed lists of what he fasted, but to put it in simple terms, he fasted meats and sweets).

After the three weeks were up, he was with a group of men, when suddenly a man appeared before him. He is described as being dressed in linen, with a belt of the finest gold around his waist. Verse 6 says his body was like chrysolite, his face like lighting, his eyes like flaming torches, his arms and legs like the gleam of burnished bronze and his voice like the sound of the multitude. It's really interesting to me that Daniel was the only one who saw the angel. The men who were with him did not see him, but they sensed that something was happening. They were filled with terror and ran to hide themselves. Daniel, the one who had set his heart to seek answers from the Lord, the one who was fasting, had his eyes opened, and as a result, he could *see* something the rest of them could only sense and dread. Fasting gives you an advantage!

The angel spoke to Daniel and told him,

> Do not be afraid, Daniel. Since the first day that you set your mind to gain understanding and to humble yourself before your God, your words were heard, and I have come in response to them. But the prince of the Persian kingdom resisted me twenty-one days. Then Michael, one of the chief princes, came to help me, because I was detained there with the king of Persia.

Now I have come to explain to you what will happen to your people in the future, for the vision concerns a time yet to come.
—DANIEL 12-14

Fasting generates activity in the Spirit—especially when we're talking about a designated fast. Daniel fasted, and God sent an answer. The answer was delayed because the enemy was fighting against it! The prince, or principality, that controlled Persia resisted what God wanted to do in and through Daniel. Daniel thought he was just asking for understanding of a vision in his fast, but what was really happening was 100-percent spiritual warfare. The delayed answer was due to the battle being waged with principalities and powers that literally controlled certain regions. Through Daniel's fasting, even the battle in the spirit realm was strengthened.

Through fasting we can bring breakthrough in the spirit—in spiritual obstructions. There are spiritual reasons as to why you have found it impossible to move forward. There are roadblocks that have been erected against the advance of your ministry, church, family or your personal journey of restoration and freedom. Through fasting, we engage in war against those roadblocks. We are battling in the spirit realm through fasting. We reap the benefits in the natural. We may not see the breakthrough in the natural immediately, but we are chipping away at those barriers in the spirit! When we cooperate with the Spirit through fasting, the effort of God is strengthened in our lives. When we cooperate through fasting we are saying, "May your kingdom come, may your will be done *here on earth*, even as it is in heaven!" His will has already been declared and established in heaven, but when we begin to cry out to God, we are cooperating and causing His will to be established here on earth! He's the one who prompts us to seek Him for answers, breakthrough or revelation.

How can we properly cooperate with heaven? We cooperate by praying, by searching the Word *and by fasting*. When someone on earth begins to cooperate with what God in heaven has declared—get ready, because something is going to break through into the natural, and God's will is going to be manifest in your earthly situation!

I remember a fast I felt prompted to go on some years ago. I sensed an urgency from the Lord to fast. So I did. The things that God spoke to me during that fast were almost beyond my ability to believe. It had to do with impossible situations in my family. When I felt a release from the fast (when I felt like I could stop fasting and resume eating), I expected those miracles to happen within 24 hours! It didn't happen like that. What I felt when I ended the fast was complete breakthrough. God will many times give you that sign in your heart—you will feel like something has been accomplished, like it's a done deal. That feeling is a sign from the Lord that something *was* accomplished. But, as it was in my case, I didn't see the fulfillment of what I felt the Lord speak to me during that fast until five years later!

Fasting, as it relates to spiritual warfare, also makes preparation for the preaching of the Word. It prepares the ground, so to speak, where you will be ministering. It is a critical element in preparation for evangelism. I often fast for services or conferences where I am scheduled to preach. I can honestly tell you that when I fast beforehand, it makes a night and day difference in the ministry. When I fast for specific ministry opportunities, I am petitioning God on behalf of the people and their needs. I am asking the Holy Spirit for a powerful outpouring and manifestations of the gifts of the Spirit. I am petitioning God for signs and wonders. I am asking God for a supernatural anointing for expressing and preaching the Word. I often pray the Word back to the Lord that He has given me to preach for that particular place. I believe fasting is effective in preparing people's hearts to receive from the Lord—and it is effective in binding the enemy in specific places so the will of the Lord may be accomplished.

Fasting is like taking a hammer and striking the barrier—striking, striking, striking *until* something breaks!

Fasting: Petitioning God

Fasting is petitioning God. It's a way of petitioning understanding. Daniel 2:22 says, "He reveals deep and hidden things; he knows what lies in darkness, and light dwells with him." Then in verse 28, we see the verse I quoted in an earlier chapter, "but there is a God in heaven who reveals mysteries."

We fast to receive revelation from God. Fasting helps us tune our ears and our spirits in to the Holy Spirit to hear, define and know what's to come. Fasting can also bring revelation of hidden things in unresolved situations.

I want to share with you one of the most amazing experiences I've ever had with fasting. Actually, it was shortly after I heard Pastor Clark teach on fasting that Sunday early in 1991.

I worked for several years as an air personality in Christian radio. In 1991, I was working for a medium market station near Houston, Texas. I loved my job. It fit me so well! It was fast-paced, required physical coordination, communication skills and focus all at once. I was happy and had moved up really quickly. There was just one problem. I knew God had called me to another type of ministry. I knew I was called to missions, and I knew that I was called to preach. All of a sudden, a few short words over the intro of a song weren't good enough anymore. I was so hungry to develop the gifts and calling of God on my life. But I didn't know how or where to start.

I was going into the last hour of my shift one night at the station. I distinctly remember turning around to put something on a shelf. When I reached for the shelf, I heard the Holy Spirit say to me, "If you're willing and obedient, I will move you out of here within 30 days and position you for full-time ministry."

Ok, pause here. That was one of those moments when I could have easily aborted something spiritually. I could have blown off that thought and relegated it to just being me rather than God. Friend, when there is a doubt in your mind as to whether something is from the Lord or not, test it! Pray over it. Fast about it!

I stopped in my tracks and said, "Lord, if this is you, confirm this to me!" Then I decided to do something that would change my life. I decided to fast.

I got my three index cards out (yes, *real* index cards—this was precomputer days!) and labeled them. I fasted for three days. I won't take time to write out all of the Scriptures the Lord gave me during that time, but let me write out some of the directive thoughts I received during those three days of fasting and prayer.

I kept hearing the word *mission* in my mind. I must've written it down a half dozen times on my card! Not only that, during that time I received a personal prophecy from a lady pastor at my church in which she said, "I just keep hearing the word *mission*—not sure what that means, but maybe you're going on a mission? Regardless, God is speaking *mission* over your life!"

I wrote down: I will live rent free—God is going to provide a place free for me. Even as I wrote it down, I felt silly. But I wrote it anyway.

The next thing I sensed was God saying He was going to put me under the leadership of a pastor who would become a mentor and spiritual father to me, whose influence would impact the rest of my life and ministry.

Next I wrote: My experience in radio will open the door, but this isn't the reason He is sending me to this next place.

Another leader prayed over me during that time and told me, "I keep seeing the word *mission*—not sure what that means to you, but…"

My mom called me one day during my fast (I had told her I was fasting and feeling like God had a change for me), and told me that she really felt like God was going to put me under the mentorship of a pastor—someone who was missions-minded. She then told me she had met a pastor of a church down in the Rio Grande Valley (south Texas on the border of Mexico) who was incredibly missions-minded, as well as a man of prayer. She said, "I really would love for you to get to visit his church sometime—it would be so neat if God put you in a church that has a pastor like that!" She told me she thought the name of the city where he pastored was called McAllen, but she wasn't sure. I got off the phone and looked up his name in a church directory I had. I was completely shocked to find that he didn't pastor in McAllen, but in a city called Mission. God had my attention! I had no idea previously there was a city named Mission.

On the fourth day after beginning the fast, I got up and

felt like whatever it God had wanted to accomplish was done. I breathed a prayer and said, "Lord—so be it! I feel like it's a done deal—confirm these things to me so I know I'm not crazy but really hearing from you!"

So, what did I do next? I headed straight for the refrigerator! I wanted food!

As soon as I opened the refrigerator door, the phone rang. It was a former boss of mine. He told me he was calling me from south Texas, close to the border of Mexico. He was the on-air manager for a new Christian music radio station there and was calling to offer me a position on the air. The position he was offering me sounded awesome and piqued my interest. So I said, "Wait a second, where did you say the station is at?"

He said, "It's in a city called McAllen, next to a town called Mission." I almost fell off the chair! I said, "What? Where!?"

He said, "McAllen. There's a smaller town next to it called Mission, but they are so close you almost can't tell the difference when you pass from one to the other."

I agreed to a visit. Even that was a miracle. I didn't have the money for the extras of the trip, and out of the blue got a refund check from my insurance company because I'd overpaid the year before! Unbelievable.

To make a long story a little bit shorter, I made the trip to interview for the position. The whole time, I kept reviewing my little index cards and praying those words back to the Lord! I knew radio was opening the door for me, but it wasn't God's ultimate purpose for sending me there. During my interview trip, I also went to visit the church of the pastor that my mom had told me about. It was an awesome church! They had a school of ministry in the church where young people who felt called into ministry were being mentored full-time.

They also had a passion for foreign missions—over 20 of their college students were missionaries in foreign countries supported solely by the youth and young adults of the church. I knew it was where I was supposed to attend!

Within 30 days after the Lord spoke to me that night in the radio station, I was making the move to Mission, Texas. I started working at the station. One of the perks I was offered in my salary was to do live ads on the air for local businesses. Air personalities can make good extra money from what are called talent fees when they personally sell a certain product or promote a business live on the air. Of course, this is a contract made between the DJ and the business owner or manager. I made a deal with a local real estate developer. He owned properties, mostly apartment complexes all over the area. How did he pay me? He gave me an apartment rent-free in exchange for on air promotions during my radio show! So there I was, in Mission, Texas, living rent-free. Just like the Lord had impressed on my heart during my fast. I still have that little index card!

Within 90 days after arriving and starting my new position, the radio station abruptly closed because of financial difficulties. The same day I found out I was out of a job, the pastor who ran the school of ministry at my church called me and said he wanted to meet with me. I told no one what had happened that morning—that I had lost my job. When I met with my pastor that afternoon he said, "Renay, the Lord spoke to me about you. I feel like it's time for you to come on staff in the school of ministry program—I want to mentor you—I feel like God wants to begin developing your ministry giftings and call. But this will require a huge step on your part. You'll have to resign from the radio station because you will be here at the church full-time. I'd like to see you start as soon as possible." *Amazing*! It was everything I could do not to weep and laugh at the same time!

To this day, I continue to reap from my mentor's influence, his ministry and what he sowed into my life during the time I spent under his leadership. It was a time where God deeply impacted my life. He changed my heart about ministry. He stirred up a hunger for the supernatural—to see the God of my fathers move and make Himself known in my life and in my generation.

Friend, do you ever stop to think about the miracles of the Bible? How the king who threw the three Hebrew children into the fiery furnace looked into the fire and saw *four* people instead of three—and none of them were burning—and how they came out without even the hint of the smell of smoke? Do you ever think about how Daniel spent a night in a den of lions, and he slept like a baby—and apparently so did the lions? Do you think about how Jesus said, "Greater things than these will *you* do because I go to my Father"? He delights in the miraculous!

God is very much alive. He has not changed. He very much wants to reveal things to us and speak to us today—the same way He has spoken to His people throughout history! One of the ways He does that is through fasting. Fasting is a Spirit-led time where you put your ear to the ground to hear what no one else is hearing, feeling or discerning! Fasting generates the miraculous.

Fasting: Sensitizing Ourselves to the Lord

Fasting is a tool to help keep us sensitized to the Lord. It brings divine alignment, which means, it helps us align ourselves in body, soul and spirit to the will of God.

Remember when the disciples couldn't cast the demons out of someone, and Jesus responded and said, "These come out only by prayer and fasting"? It seems to me, then, that fasting should be a part of our normal spiritual regimen. I believe Jesus was saying that a lifestyle of fasting brings a recognized authority and stature spiritually when confronting the enemy. I've often wondered why? I think it's because fasting helps us in the area of holiness. We have authority spiritually because God through Jesus delegated it to us. But holiness—holiness is a result of sanctification—sanctification is a process of ongoing submission to the inner work of the Holy Spirit in all areas of our lives in order to become more like Jesus. Holiness gives us courage in the face of the enemy.

Fasting sensitizes us not only to the Lord, but also to others. Isaiah 58 tells us how important our actions towards the needs of others are. Fasting should activate something within us as it relates to the needs of people and the heart of God.

When a car is out of alignment, you will have a constant tug-of-war in the driver's seat. The car will pull to one side or the other. The driver can never loosen their grip on the wheel even ever so slightly because the car will not maintain a straight course—it's basically a struggle between the one wanting to steer and the vehicle. Now, if someone aligns the front end of the vehicle and brings the tires into balance, it will drive like a different machine. You go from feeling like you are in a run-down jalopy to a luxury car. Why? Because all of the systems and mechanics are working together properly—one area is no longer working against and weakening the function of another area.

Our lives work pretty much the same way. We are body, soul and spirit. Our body has to do with, well, the physical part of us! The soul is the mind, the will and the emotions (the flesh or carnal man). Our spirit or our emotions and thoughts directly influence our will. The spirit is that part of us where we are able to connect with God eternally. It's the entryway of God into man. It's the part of us that is most sensitive to God, because our spirit was designed to house Him.

If our soul is not aligned with the Spirit of God, under His control and influence, we will be under the control of the soul (unrestrained thoughts, emotions and vulnerable will). For this reason, Proverbs 4:23 says above all else to guard your heart, because out of your heart you will determine your life's choices and life view. Do you know what the word *heart* means in the Hebrew in that verse? It means mind, will, intellect and emotions. Above all else, guard your mind, will and emotions! A call of God and a passion for His work will not alone guarantee that you will accomplish the things God has called you to do. If you do not develop your inner life—your mind, your will and your emotions—if they are not brought under the alignment of the spirit, your life and journey will be riddled with delay and setbacks. As Christians we have a tendency to get really spiritual about a lot of things—but we fail to recognize the great need and responsibility we have to be spiritual in our attitudes, emotions and inner life. Galations 5:22 tells us we should be bearing fruit in our attitudes and even in our personalities!

When we are aligned spiritually, it brings healing to our body, our relationships and emotions.

So, how do we keep our lives aligned to the will of God and the example of Jesus? We do it through daily relationship with Him in prayer and in the Word. We wash ourselves in the water of the Word. We think on the goodness of God, and we worship Him, acknowledging Him in our daily lives. But another regimen we need to include in our spiritual lives is fasting. When we fast, we are aligning our soul. We are aligning our body. And, without a doubt, we are strengthening our spirit. When all of those areas begin to function together—when one area is not working against and weakening the other, there will be an amazing transformation in your daily life and walk with God.

CHAPTER 6

APPOINTED AND ANOINTED TO REIGN

How many times have we heard that David was a man after God's own heart? He was. His life serves as an incredible example to us in so many ways.

So when I dove into I Kings 1 and 2 and saw that he almost abdicated the throne, it took me by surprise.

To *abdicate* means to give up duties and obligations; thereby, giving up power and position, as well. When we refuse or fail to take up our spiritual position as children of God (co-heirs with Christ), we immediately abdicate our dominion to the devil.

On the other hand, to *reign* means to possess or exercise sovereign power; it also means to prevail.

Keeping those two definitions in mind, let's jump into the scene found in I Kings 1 and 2.

King David was nearing the end of his life. He was ripe with age, and had accomplished much for God and for Israel. He had, with character and uprightness before God, even dealt with personal tragedy and failure. He deserved some rest, right?

In the first chapter we find the king resting on his laurels. OK, well, sort of. He was *very* old, the Bible says, and he was constantly cold. I guess his blood was thin. His servants couldn't keep him warm even by piling covers on top of him. So, they sought a beautiful young lady to come and keep him warm and comfortable. They did not have a sexual relationship; she simply took care of him. He was, as we would contextualize it in our terms, enjoying the golden years of retirement. It was his time to relax and unplug.

While King David was unplugging a bit in his final days, the rest of the kingdom was staying quite active. Outside the palace walls, life went on.

During this time, one of David's sons, Adonijah, younger brother of Absalom, was busy taking full advantage of the benefits of being son of the king. Frequently, he would prepare all of the King's chariots and stallions and would parade around the city and countryside in them. He loved the pomp of it all. He loved the power and the attention. His father never questioned nor corrected his behavior.

Knowing that his father would soon die, and that no successor had been named to the throne, Adonijah said to himself, *I will be king!* So, he started a personal campaign trying to generate support for his plan.

He went to all the Who's Who of the kingdom. After invoking their favor and endorsement, he invited religious figureheads, all of his brothers except for one, as well as important leaders of the kingdom to a huge banquet that he would give in his own honor celebrating his ascent to the throne as king in his father's stead.

It's interesting to note that there were four important people left off of his invitation list: His father, King David; Zadok, the priest; Nathan, the prophet; and Solomon, Adonijah's brother.

Meanwhile, back at the palace, David rested in his quarters enjoying the satisfaction of past victories. Yet, his God-given calling and subsequent responsibilities had not expired nor gone into retirement with him! He still had a territory and a kingdom to rule and reign.

When Adonijah's party began, Nathan the prophet paid a visit to Bathsheba, Solomon's mother. He said,

> Have you not heard that Adonijah, the son of Haggith, has become king, and our lord David knows nothing about it? Now then, let me advise you how you can save your own life and the life of your son Solomon. Go in to King David and say to him, 'My lord the king, did you not swear to me your servant: "Surely Solomon your son shall be king after me, and he will sit on my throne?" Why then has Adonijah become king?' While you are still there talking to the king, I will come in and add my word to what you have said.
>
> –I KINGS 1:11-14

So, Bathsheba went in and spoke to the king. She told him everything Nathan had instructed her to say, and she added,

> My lord the king, the eyes of all Israel are on you, to learn from you who will sit on the throne of my lord the king after him.

Otherwise, as soon as my lord the king is laid to rest with his ancestors, I and my son Solomon will be treated as criminals.

–I KINGS 1:20-21

Nathan and Bathsheba both realized what the consequences would be if David did not act: It would cost Bathsheba and Solomon their lives. Our actions, good and bad, have a domino effect. Their consequences can echo for generations.

As soon as she finished, Nathan came in to see the king. He confirmed everything Bathsheba had said. He told the king that even at that moment, Adonijah was hosting a festival celebrating his new position as king. Adonijah's festival had all the makings of a true spiritual celebration: He sacrificed hundreds of cattle and sheep; he had well-known religious people celebrating with him—it had the look and feel of something authentic—but it wasn't!

The king then took an oath:

As surely as the LORD lives, who has delivered me out of every trouble, I will surely carry out this very day what I swore to you by the LORD, the God of Israel: Solomon your son shall be king after me, and he will sit on my throne in my place.

–1 KINGS 1:29-30

So David *appointed* Solomon as king.

When his servants heard David's declaration they responded saying, "Amen! May the LORD, the God of my lord the king, so declare it. As the LORD was with my lord the king, so may he be with Solomon to make his throne *even greater than the throne of my lord King David!*" (verses 36 and 37)

The king told his servants to call Solomon and to summon

Zadok the priest. He instructed his servants to place Solomon on his donkey and instructed Zadok the priest and Nathan the prophet to lead him to Gihon to the sacred tent. He instructed them to anoint Solomon with oil there, and afterwards, to sound the trumpet and declare, "Long live King Solomon!" He told them that Solomon should sit on his throne and reign in his place because "I have *appointed* him ruler…" (1 Kings 1:35)

Nathan, Zadok, and Solomon did as David had instructed them. They went down to the sacred tent with Solomon seated on the king's donkey. The priest went into the sacred tent and brought out a horn filled with oil. He poured the oil over Solomon's head and, before the Lord, *anointed* him king. They sounded the trumpet and began to shout, "Long live King Solomon!" All of the people began to shout it as well, and went up playing their flutes and instruments. The noise of their rejoicing was such that the ground shook because of it!

Meanwhile, Adonijah and his guests were just finishing their feast. On hearing the sound of the trumpet, a man named Joab (a man who had history with King David) said, "What's the meaning of all of the noise in the city?"

The reply?

Our lord King David has made Solomon king. The king has sent with him Zadok the priest, Nathan the prophet, Benaiah son of Jehoiada, the Kerethites and the Pelethites, and they have put him on the king's mule, and Zadok the priest and Nathan the prophet have anointed him king at Gihon. From there they have gone up cheering, and the city resounds with it. That's the noise you hear. Moreover, Solomon has taken his seat on the royal throne. Also, the royal officials have come to congratulate our lord King David, saying, 'May your God make Solomon's name more famous than yours and his throne greater than yours!' And the king bowed in worship on his bed and said, 'Praise be to the LORD, the God of Israel, who has allowed my eyes to see a successor on my throne today'.

—1 KINGS 1:43-48

You can imagine Adonijah's reaction! His party was over— His charade had ended. He threw himself on Solomon's mercy.

At this point, Solomon is sitting on the throne. You would think that everything was well established. But that wasn't the case. He had been *appointed* by the king, and *anointed* by the priest and prophet, but the kingdom wasn't yet secured under his leadership.

As the time of David's death drew near, he summoned Solomon. He spoke to his son (1 Kings 2:1), charging him to keep God's ways and commands. In his charge to Solomon, David made sure that Solomon understood that the consequences of his future behavior would have a direct bearing on God's promises towards David being fulfilled. A promise was made to David—but its fulfillment was directly connected to the next generation. If the next generation carried on honoring God, then the multi-generational promise made to the previous generation would be fulfilled. If not, then a spiritual inheritance would be held up until someone in a future generation picked up the mantle and began to obey the Lord once more, which would reinstate God's favor and blessing.

The next thing David addressed was critical to establishing the kingdom in Solomon's hands. He spoke to Solomon about two people who were enemies of the throne: Joab and Shimei. They were longtime enemies of David.

Joab had shed the innocent blood of two commanders in Israel's army while it was under David's command, in essence, bringing blood guilt to David and his household. David admonishes Solomon to use his wisdom in dealing with Joab, but to not let Joab die unpunished. The second man named was Shimei. Shimei had betrayed David by calling down bitter curses upon him at a crucial time in David's reign. David tells Solomon not to consider Shimei innocent, but rather to punish him, telling Solomon that, in his wisdom, he will know what to do with him.

It's really important to understand that David is warning Solomon of two enemies who had wreaked havoc during his *own* tenure as king. The warning was this: These enemies will become enemies in *your* generation if you do not deal with them.

Soon after having this conversation with Solomon, David died.

Solomon immediately began to deal with the enemies of his father. Upon hearing that Solomon was cleaning house, so to speak, Joab fled to the tent of the Lord and took hold of the altar. When the man assigned to strike him down (Benaiah) found him there, he ordered Joab to come out. Joab refused and said, "No, I will die here!" Benaiah reported this to Solomon, and Solomon said, "OK, according to his own words—so be it! He will die there!" Solomon sent Benaiah back to Joab and he struck him down and killed him (1 Kings 2:30-31).

Next there was the issue of Shimei. Solomon summoned Shimei to himself. He told Shimei to build a house in

Jerusalem and to stay there. He then told him, "If you ever leave and cross the border, you will die and your blood will be on your own head." Shimei agreed to this (anything, I'm sure, to save his head at the moment!). Shimei stayed put for a long time. But, three years later, two of his slaves ran off. What did Shimei do? He went after them. They had left Jerusalem and crossed the border. He crossed over and brought them back with him to Jerusalem. When King Solomon heard of this, he summoned Shimei again. He rebuked him and reminded him of the binding contract they had between them. Shimei had disobeyed and broken his vow. The king then gave the order to Benaiah to strike Shimei down. He did so, and Shimei died (1 Kings 2:36-46a).

The last sentence of chapter 2 is the most powerful phrase of the whole story. The Bible says in verse 46, "The kingdom was now established *in* Solomon's hands." Solomon did not wait on God to do something miraculous that would rid the kingdom of its enemies. No. Solomon understood *his* role in seeing God's will accomplished in his life! Solomon acted! David had encouraged his son to call upon the gift of God within him, which was the gift of wisdom. The story shows us how Solomon acted in wisdom regarding Joab and Shimei. He literally let their own words hang them, so to speak. It was genius! But it was also intentional. The kingdom was established through Solomon's own hands. How? He cooperated with God by walking in and administrating the spiritual authority and position that he had been assigned and anointed for.

Throughout the course of this book, I've been talking about one powerful thing: Overcoming! For many of us, that means we must overcome things in our lineage if we desire to leave a legacy. It means refusing a repeat performance in our lives of the sins of the father. And by the sins of the father, I hope you understand by now that I am not referring exclusively to our biological fathers, but rather the spirit of previous generations: Their attitudes, their spiritual posture before the Lord, their failures. For some, overcoming means choosing to pursue a path of healing: refusing to allow wounds to define them — rejecting the role of victim. For still others, it means confronting personal strongholds—refusing to accept their current state as a permanent status.

But all of that boils down to one thing: *Overcoming* in order to establish the Kingdom of God in our lives and in our generation. At the end of my life, will Jesus be left standing where I have lived? When my body dies, will the life I lived continue to bear fruit? Will I have set up the next generation for tragedy or triumph?

The story of David and Solomon mirrors the life of every believer. All of the players we see in this story are players that exist in the journey of our lives. There are critical elements we can see at work in every paragraph in this story. The same holds true in our own spiritual journey. There are critical elements we need to be aware of. And, then, there's the most important element of all: The assignment and anointing of God upon our lives. Recognizing the sacredness of our position as children of God, and our shared authority as co-heirs with Jesus is paramount in winning spiritual battles in our lifetime.

We've talked about lineage and turning our life around, but now the question is this: Do you want to leave a spiritual legacy?

Drawing from the story of David and Solomon, here are 10 characteristics of a person of legacy:

1. A person of legacy wouldn't be caught dead with their mantle on!

A person who wants to leave a spiritual legacy, understands that their mantle was never intended for use as a grave cloth. They understand that a mantle is a multi-generational cloak!

David ran the risk of dying with his mantle still on his shoulders. A mantle that goes down to the grave is an abdication of spiritual rights and authority. A legacy leaver will not retire their spiritual position with age: They will finish strong, and they will intentionally pass on their mantle!

2. A person of legacy will always invest in the next generation

People of legacy have an eye for the future. They live with the end in mind. Had David not intentionally appointed his son Solomon as his successor, David himself would have been displaced by Adonijah, and he would have destined Solomon and Bathsheba to a life lived within the confines of an illegal transaction. Invest in spiritual sons and daughters—set them up for reigning, not captivity!

3. A person of legacy refuses to move in a competitive spirit

In verses 47 and 48 of the first chapter of this story, we see a great example of this. Upon hearing David appoint Solomon as king, David's servants said,

> May your God make Solomon's name *more famous than yours and his throne GREATER than yours!* And the king bowed in worship upon his bed, and said, 'Praise be to the LORD, God

of Israel, Who has allowed my eyes to see a successor on my throne today!'

What an example David left us! Many leaders would have reacted in a totally different way. David could have said, "Hey wait a minute! You're *my* servant! I don't want you to like him more than me! You shouldn't wish that someone else's throne be greater than mine!" But, he didn't react that way. Instead, what did he do? He bowed down on his bed and praised God! Why? David refused to move in a competitive or jealous spirit regarding the things of God. He understood they were God's and not his! He understood that the victories of his son were directly attached to the seeds he'd sown in his own generation. We need to encourage increase and an expectancy of greater things in the next generation—encourage it with intentional blessing! David *rejoiced in it*!

David also knew that Solomon's role would be different than his own. David desired to build a temple for the Lord, but God wouldn't allow him to. Instead, the Lord told David He had chosen Solomon for that task. God help us, as leaders, to not commit spiritual abortion because of a jealous or competitive spirit towards the younger generation! When we raise up sons and daughters in the Lord, they are not ours to keep. Healthy spiritual parents understand the importance of releasing their spiritual children with a blessing (in attitude and support) when it's time for them to fulfill their own call. Some of the most wounded people in the ministry whom I've ever sat and counseled are spiritual sons and daughters whose father or mother turned against them when they sought their blessing and support to begin pursuing the fulfillment of their own dream.

I have said this to young people that I've mentored: "I want you to go further than I ever dreamed of going! My prayer is that one day, I will see a blur flying past me, and it will be *you*—may you go further than I ever dreamed!"

4. People of legacy have a *today* mentality

David said, "...I will surely carry out *today* what I swore to you by the LORD, the God of Israel: Solomon your son shall be king after me, and he will sit on my throne in my place."

A person of legacy is able to recognize critical moments in God's timeline. They understand the need to act today, rather than run the risk of delay and detour.

5. A person of legacy will seek out and follow the authentic

It was prophesied in the 1906 Azusa Street Revival that: "In the last days three things will happen in the great Pentecostal Movement: 1) There will be an over-emphasis on power, *rather than on righteousness.* 2) There will be an overemphasis on praise, *to a God to whom they no longer pray.* 3) There will be an overemphasis on the gifts of the Spirit — *rather than on the Lordship of Christ"* (*Get Out Of The Box*, Richard Laux and Ben Lunis. p.477).

I believe we are living in the last days before Christ returns. And, because of the times, we desperately need to guard our hearts and our relationship with the Lord. Why? Because not everything that looks spiritual is. Just because something is good, doesn't mean it's of God.

Look at Adonijah: He threw the kingdom party of the decade; he sacrificed hundreds of animals; everyone who was anyone important in the kingdom was throwing in their support for what he was doing! He was the golden boy of the moment—the flash-in-the-pan guy! Yet none of what was happening had been sanctioned by heaven! There were power players who attended his party attempting to promote him to a level of spiritual leadership without God having anything to do with it. Apparently, he was a talented guy. But talent is no substitute for anointing. Talent and gifting without anointing will only get you so far. There was praise and an abundance of music, yet no one had bothered to stop and pray and inquire of the Lord! There was absolutely no evidence of Adonijah having a heart after God. He had neither been appointed by the king, nor anointed by the priest and the prophet!

And then there was Solomon. He was the only brother who was not invited to the party. He wasn't very flashy. He wasn't very popular. The important people didn't flock to him. He was virtually anonymous. He didn't follow Adonijah and the Who's Who of the kingdom. Instead, he obeyed his father and followed an old priest and an old prophet down to the sacred tent. He didn't ride mounted on a royal stallion or a chariot from his father's palace. No. He went on a donkey. And there, at the sacred tent, without any fanfare or public support, the old priest and prophet anointed him king. Solomon resisted the religious trend, and instead followed the authentic.

Remember the question that Joab asked when Adonijah's party was winding down? "What's the meaning of all the noise in the city?" It was the sound of *authenticity*! The enemy recognizes it! When the authentic took place, it exposed deception.

In today's Christian ministry culture, it would be easy to fall into the popularity trap: The feeling that one has to position themselves with the Who's Who of the Kingdom in order to be able to ascend to a place of influence in this generation. Don't fall into that trap, friend. Don't run to the party—wait for the oil to be poured out! Follow the authentic. Value true anointing and refined character over talent and ability. True anointing comes from one source: the secret place. There's still a King, Priest and a Prophet pouring out the anointing of the Holy Spirit on those willing to break away from the crowd.

6. Legacy leavers value the secret place

Adonijah wanted the position and benefits without the *intimacy*—without a relationship with the priest and prophet (Jesus). He preferred working the system rather than humbly going to the throne room.

There is *no substitute* for *true anointing*! And it only comes from the secret place. You cannot truly administrate the Kingdom, and leave a spiritual inheritance, without it! You cannot get there without the true anointing—it's not found in the fanfare of men, but only in the secret place with God.

People of legacy desire the secret place more than the public place. They learn the value of time in prayer and private worship. They long for it because the oil that flows from there has marked them! They are not solely after polished sermons; they want to bring a word from the Lord. They leave you wanting to be closer to Jesus, and to act more like Him. They are those whose lives are talked about long after they are gone from this earth.

7. A person of legacy is marked by humility

The differences between David and Adonijah were many. David rode mounted on his donkey. His son, Adonijah, preferred the royal chariots and stallions. The difference between the two was one thing — humility.

Jesus came into Jerusalem riding a donkey. David commanded his servants to set Solomon upon his donkey when it was time for the priest and prophet to anoint him. A person of legacy will always be marked by humility. They will not draw attention to themselves, but to their message and to the person of Jesus.

8. Legacy leavers are agents of change

People who leave a legacy are determined to exchange cries of victimization for divine declaration. They understand the power of declaring the word of the Lord over their generation.

By the time Solomon had been anointed king, there were already scores of people crying out, "Long live King Adonijah!" But did that discourage Nathan and Zadok from following through with the decree of King David? Absolutely not! They understood the power of divine decree! When someone declared the decree of the king, the tide turned! Nathan and Zadok were agents of change.

Legacy leavers facilitate change through their faith and their declaration in the face of overwhelming circumstances! They grab hold of the promises of God and go against the current of what is happening in the natural realm! They usher in a turning of the tide simply by their unflinching obedience and faith in the decrees of the King.

9. A person of legacy understands the human element in divine things

Miracles usually have two elements: The God-element and

the human-element. In other words, God ordains something, but He also ordains *someone* to carry it out!

God's plan for Solomon's reign started way before Solomon was born! God gifted Solomon with divine wisdom. He was the wisest man who ever lived. God gifted him with wisdom for a specific *purpose*.

I can't tell you the amount of times I have prayed, "Oh God, I ask that You do this" or "do that" or "(fill in the blank)."But one day, I had to adjust the way I was praying! In fact, it was when I was really seeking God and the Word about principles of spiritual warfare. I had been praying that God bind the enemy. All of the sudden I felt like the Lord said, "No, you bind him." Huh? Yeah. That's what I felt! And then it made sense to me: There's nothing more God can do to increase the authority on my life in order that I might be able to better administrate the Kingdom (work the works of Jesus, accomplish the will of God, etc.). He's done His part. I began to understand that even in binding the enemy I had a role to play! God already bound the enemy. But now I have to stand my ground and uphold the law, so to speak! I have to declare the Word with my mouth! I have to back up the Word in my life with right and holy living. That's my part. Miracles work the same way! When we understand that God's part has already been established, we will begin to understand the authority that He's placed in us to carry out His heart and His will in any given circumstance.

Solomon didn't wait on God to strike down the two men who were threatening the kingdom. God had appointed and anointed Solomon to reign over that kingdom. It was Solomon's job to administrate the kingdom! God had gifted him to be able to deal with those enemies. And he did it. And the

Bible says that because of his own actions, the "kingdom was now established in Solomon's hands." The word *in* actually implies *through* in several versions. Through Solomon's hands (hands that were appointed and anointed), the kingdom was established.

10. Legacy leavers stand up when others sit down

People of legacy are courageous. They go against the grain.

Bathsheba and Nathan had the courage to stand up when the majority of the city was sitting down to a feast at the house of a usurper. They dared to speak up when no one else in the kingdom, including David's closest men and confidants, would. Because they dared to stand up when others sat down, the course of history was changed, and a legacy was saved.

CHAPTER 7

WALKING IN THE OPPOSITE SPIRIT

In Judges 6 we see a picture of a whole nation of people living beneath their potential, and definitely, beneath their calling. Other people groups they had once conquered now plundered them year after year, for seven years. Each year, the Israelites would sow their seeds and work their fields, bringing them to a place of harvest. But when it was finally time to harvest and enjoy the abundance of their labor, their enemies would come and set up camp surrounding them. The Midianites and other enemies of Israel were so numerous their camels could not even be numbered. Each year, when it was time for the Israelites to harvest, their enemies moved in. They purposefully ruined any leftovers. They would even carry off their sheep and other herds of livestock. It was an awful reality to live.

So, what had opened the door and given their enemies

permission to enter? Gideon's father's generation opened the door to the enemy when they disobeyed the Lord. After seven years of laboring in vain and being robbed of their harvest because of their disobedience, Israel finally began to wake up. But it's interesting to note they didn't cry out to God in repentance — they didn't recognize they themselves had opened the door to all of this tragedy — they cried out because of their misery! God allowed their enemies to push them towards repentance and crying out to Him for help.

And how did God respond? He sent an unnamed prophet to them. Prophets show up when something needs to be clarified! They also show up when correction is needed. Before we can receive deliverance from our sin, we have to recognize what it is we did wrong so that we can correct it! The prophet showed up and brought clarity to the situation. He brought a clear word from the Lord — he told the Israelites why they were in the situation they were in.

A prophet always precedes a deliverer. When a prophet comes — or when God sends a Word from the Lord — that's always a sign that deliverance is in the making! John the Baptist prepared the way for the Messiah. And, in this passage of Scripture in Judges 6, the prophet preceded the raising up of a deliverer named Gideon.

Gideon was the son of Joash. Joash had the same spirit of everyone else of his era. He went with the flow. Everyone had turned to idols, and Joash was no different. In fact, he constructed a prominent altar to Baal on his own property. But Joash was also no different than everyone else in that he and his family were also living hand to mouth because of that open door.

After the prophet came and brought a word from the Lord,

the Angel of the Lord then showed up on the scene. He appeared to young Gideon as he was threshing wheat in a winepress, hiding out from the Midianites. This encounter would be a game changer for Gideon.

The Angel of the Lord appears to Gideon and says, "The LORD is with you, valiant warrior!" I can almost see the look on Gideon's face! I imagine him turning around and looking behind him to see who the angel is *really* talking to. Here's this young guy, hiding out from the enemy in a winepress trying to thresh just enough wheat for his family to eke out their daily meals with, and the Angel of the Lord shows up and calls him a valiant warrior and tells him the Lord is with him?

Gideon responded and said,

> "But sir," Gideon replied, "if the LORD is with us, why has all this happened to us? Where are all his wonders that our fathers told us about when they said, 'Did not the LORD bring us up out of Egypt?' But now the LORD has abandoned us and put us into the hand of Midian.
>
> –JUDGES 6:13

Gideon responds not with a personal response, but rather with a corporate one. He said, "If the LORD is with *us…*" When we've seen disaster touch our father's generation, sometimes it's hard to believe for a different outcome in our own. It's almost as if Gideon was saying, "If I'm not seeing that God is corporately with us, then how can I personally believe for this?"

In the timeline of the story, it was harvest time when the angel showed up. That's why Gideon was down in the winepress: It was time for history to repeat itself. The enemies of

Israel were already gathering and setting up camp around the fields of the Israelites. Gideon knew what was coming — a complete plunder of everything they had worked for. That's one of the reasons he responds so strongly to the angel of the Lord: He was complaining! I love the divine dissatisfaction or complaint that we see in Gideon. He wasn't whining — he was disillusioned because he knew there was more to life — he knew there was a greater inheritance they were entitled to than what they were currently living! He began to cite the miracles that God had worked for generations past. He'd heard the stories from the lips of his ancestors. He was asking, "Where is He now? Where is His favor? Where are the signs and wonders?"

Sometimes the complaint and dissatisfaction we feel inside is divinely placed — God put it there! *Like Gideon, God allowed that divine dissatisfaction to rise up within so it would motivate and push Gideon towards God's promises of greater things, towards the benefits of God* (Psa. 103:2-6)! God used a *divine complaint* to inspire a young man to rise up and change the course of a nation!

When Gideon realized he'd seen the Angel of the Lord face to face, the Lord spoke to him. The Lord sent Gideon to get a bull from his father's herd in order to prepare it as a sacrifice. The bull that he commanded him to take was a bull that was seven years old. The Lord then commanded Gideon to tear down the altar to Baal that his father had built and to also cut down the Asherah pole beside it and use it as wood for the fire. God told Gideon to sacrifice the seven-year-old bull on the altar.

I love what God was doing for this young man who longed to change the course of his life, his family and his nation. God told him to sacrifice something that represented the seven-year captivity Israel had been under. God was allowing this young man to take hold of the limits of his birthmark and annihilate those limits on the altar! He was giving Gideon a visual of what was happening in the spirit!

What was happening? A young man decided to *walk in the opposite spirit.* He decided to go against the grain and close the door his father's generation had opened to the enemy.

What does it mean to *walk in the opposite spirit?*

When I moved to Thailand and first began driving there, it was a challenge on several levels. First of all, the steering wheel is on the right side of the vehicle instead of on the left. Secondly, in Thailand you drive on the left side of the road instead of on the right. And, finally, there's the craziness of having to watch out for every type of vehicle known to mankind on the roadways: Tuk-tuks (three-wheeled, open-air vehicles), thousands of motorcycles, mini-trucks, big trucks, food carts pushed or pulled by vendors, etc. I remember one time pulling out of a side road onto a main road and almost getting stepped on — by an elephant! Yes, an elephant in downtown Bangkok!

The most difficult part of driving in Thailand was definitely the one-way roads or divided roads. I would invariably pull into the right side of a divided avenue instead of the left side, thus heading right into oncoming traffic! Imagine a huge avenue with tons of lanes — all one way. Imagine rush-hour traffic on steroids and you now have a good mental picture of what it's like to drive in Bangkok at any time of the day! Now imagine one person pulling into the center lane of that one-way avenue going the wrong way. Do you know what happened when I would accidentally head the wrong way up a one-way avenue? Horns were honking. Cars cut off to the right and swerved to the left. But, no one crashed into me (thankfully). It was like the parting of the Red Sea — with me driving right up the middle unscathed! I effectively interrupted the entire flow of traffic!

Walking in the opposite spirit is just like that! It's like entering the wrong way up a one-way avenue. It interrupts the flow of the enemy. It effectively ruins the momentum he has built up over the course of generations. When one person decides to turn around and walk differently — going against the grain, there is a holy interruption that begins to take place!

When Gideon turned around and began to walk the wrong way in a one-way generation, the enemy was not happy! Gideon caused a stir in Israel! He walked in the opposite spirit — instead of honoring Baal's altar, he tore it down. His father had built it up: Gideon destroyed it. His father had erected an Asherah pole next to it. Gideon walked in the opposite spirit: He cut it down. The angel had encountered Gideon hiding out in a winepress trying to preserve just enough harvest to get by on. But when God inspired Gideon through divine dissatisfaction to want *more* than enough, Gideon jumped out of the winepress and began to identify the attitudes and actions that had led him, his family, and his nation to the point of captivity in which they found themselves. Then, he began to walk in the opposite spirit in order to undo those things and reestablish the blessing of God.

When Gideon did a U-turn and went against the current, the Bible says the Spirit of the Lord came upon him and he sounded a trumpet, calling others to arms with him.

Thirty-two thousand men gathered alongside Gideon (vs. 34)! He provoked a generational turnaround. Do you see the chain reaction that can take place when just one person begins to walk in the opposite spirit?

Friend, this is what happens when we take that first step in reestablishing the blessing of God in our lives, families, and even in our nations. I think about the rich spiritual inheritance that I have. My great-grandmother, Nanny, was the first person in our family tree who acknowledged Jesus as her Lord and Savior. She was the first one to be baptized in the Holy Spirit. After being baptized in the Holy Spirit, the whole family thought she was crazy — until they had their own personal experience and began to follow Jesus as well! Nanny and her two sisters, as young single girls, began to preach brush arbor meetings in the woods of central Texas. God used them powerfully in signs and wonders. They planted churches. I've preached in churches they planted as young women. The whole family was affected by Nanny's decision to turn around and walk in the opposite spirit. The course of our family lineage did an about-face. It was a total 180! The momentum shifted from an ungodly course, to a godly heritage. I can picture that family line: Nanny, Aunt Clara, Auntie and other members of my family tree. Their lives have impacted my life.

But you know what? I can also see a shift that came after them. There were other members of our family, after Nanny and her sisters were gone, who did not continue walking with the Lord. Their behavior also had an impact — a negative one. There came a point in my life where I felt like I was Gideon, down in a winepress just trying to survive. I wasn't even thinking about abundance, I was just trying to keep my head above water! An ungodly momentum, like a strong tide that sweeps you up and carries you where you don't want to go, was strongly influencing my life. I had even ignorantly cooperated with it. I felt like Gideon felt. If the angel of the Lord had appeared to me, I would have said, "If the Lord is with us, then why are these things happening? Where is the God of the stories that my Nanny, Aunt Clara and Auntie told me? I used to sit at their feet, literally, and beg them to tell me stories of the miracles He performed through them! If He is with us, where are those things? Why am I not seeing those things in my family and in my own life?"

At a time in my life where I felt like I absolutely could not go on without answers and without a complete change in the direction in which my life was headed, God put a divine dissatisfaction inside of me. I wanted to see the God of my fathers move and deliver in my own life and in the life of my family! I began to cry out to Him—and He answered me. He helped me to identify attitudes and different areas of my life that needed an about-face. He gave me courage to turn into the enemy's on-coming traffic, and enter the wrong way down a one-way avenue! I began to see immediate changes in my life when I purposed to interrupt the enemy's flow.

Walking in the opposite spirit means taking measured steps that lead to a 180-degree turnaround. These steps result in divine order being reestablished in your life. What is divine order? Divine order happens when the attitudes and actions of our life line up with the person of Jesus and the Word of God. It means bringing all areas of our lives under the submission of Christ. I think of this concept as an unobstructed flow of the Spirit. That's the goal: That there will be no obstructions that delay, detour or detain the favor and flow of God's Spirit in and through your life.

If, for instance, you have never been generous or never honored God in tithing and offerings, walking in the opposite spirit would mean making up your mind to begin honoring God by tithing, and to be the most generous person who has ever lived! By so doing, you are breaking the influence of the enemy over your life, and you are opening the door to God's blessing! You might think, 'But I don't have a lot of money to give'. The widow in Mark 12:41-44 demonstrates that generosity is measured by the attitude of the heart, rather than by the sum of what you have to give.

If you have struggled with resentment or an offended spirit, and it has caused you to work against others instead of coming alongside them and cooperating, walking in the opposite spirit would mean a commitment to come alongside and offer support. The enemy begins to loose his grip when you stop cooperating with him!

Maybe you are a minister, and you have struggled with a competitive spirit towards other ministers in your city or area. Break the devil's stronghold of division by reaching out to other ministers whom you have avoided and be intentional in supporting their event or project. You'll be shocked at the turnaround in your own life and ministry! Make someone else's dream happen, and God will take care of yours!

Walking in the opposite spirit — Jesus did it. He changed the course of the world.

Be the pivot point for change. Ask the Holy Spirit to help you identify areas where the enemy has built up momentum — and then jump in and enter the wrong way up his one-way street. Interrupt him! Mess up his flow! Don't do what the enemy wants—do the opposite!

Change does not come easily. It does not happen magically. But it *is* possible. By making the right choices, and using the right God-given tools, the direction of your life, your family, and even the course of a generation can be changed. If that sounds like a lot of hype to you, just remember Gideon. A corporate victory always starts with *one*.

You are just 180-degrees away from a total turnaround!

Final Reflections

Every single chapter in this book has been a point of passage in my own journey from brokenness and despair, to healing and restoration.

You see, I understand what it is to feel broken and labeled. I know what it's like to believe that I would never be able to change, or, worse, that I was destined for failure spiritually and relationally. I can relate to feeling like a grasshopper in the face of my giants.

The journey to restoration and overcoming is a partnership. We cooperate with God as we walk in relationship with Him. He heals layer by layer by sending a word, whether through a word of prophecy or a word-from-the-Lord sermon that brings revelation and breakthrough to your life, your mind and emotions. Those will be God-moments—it will be *Him* doing the work in you. This is what the Israelites experienced as they crossed the Red Sea. They didn't fight. They just walked. God spoke to them through Moses and said,

> Do not be afraid. Stand firm and you will see the deliverance the LORD will bring you today. The Egyptians you see today you will never see again. The LORD will *fight for you*; you need only to be still.
>
> –Exodus 14:13-14

Then there are times when *you* will have to fight. God told the Israelites to fight when entering into Jericho because God had given them the city. God called David to fight. God called Gideon to fight! Many times the fights were against all odds. God reduced the number of Gideon's army to 300 men—down from 32,000. It was an impossible fight! The numbers were lopsided. But you have to figure in the God-factor. If God has called you to move forward (and He has)—if God has said you will defeat the enemies of your past and your future (and He has)—you will prevail against the enemy! You've been appointed and anointed for this journey!

It doesn't matter what face your enemy has: addiction, abuse, sexual immorality, abandonment, fear, poverty, or the occult. Whatever it is—God is greater. Greater is He that is in you, than he that is in the world. You have been appointed and anointed to defeat that enemy and drive him out of territory that rightfully belongs to you. It's a fight! But God is fighting for you, and God is fighting with you! May God give you supernatural strength and encouragement as you dare to confront strongholds in order to change the course of your life and future generations!

For information or comments:
renaywest@earthlink.net
www.renaywest.com

Se terminó de imprimir en el mes de septiembre de 2012 en Grancharoff
Impresores, Tapalqué 5868, C1440AET, Ciudad Autónoma de Buenos Aires.